A Vegetarian Diet

A Vegetarian Diet
What It Is; How To Make It Healthful and Enjoyable

By Shirley T. Moore, Ph.D., and Mary P. Byers, M.A.
Loma Linda University, Loma Linda, California

Published by
Woodbridge Press Publishing Company
Santa Barbara, California 93111

Published by

Woodbridge Press Publishing Company
Post Office Box 6189
Santa Barbara, California 93111

Library of Congress Card Number: 77-087548

International Standard Book Number: 0-912800-48-8

Published simultaneously in the United States and Canada

Printed in the United States of America

Library of Congress Cataloging in Publication Data

Moore, Shirley T.
  A vegetarian diet.

  1. Vegetarianism. 2. Vegetarian cookery.
I. Byers, Mary P., joint author. II. Title.
TX392.M83   613.2'6   77-87548
ISBN 0-912800-48-8

Photography, Elwyn Spaulding

Table of Contents

Acknowledgments

Many persons have helped us produce this book. Among those whose valued counsel and careful editing contributed to its scientific and technical accuracy are U.D. Register, Irma Vyhmeister, Lydia Sonnenberg, Eva Crites, and Ruth Brown, Oliver Miller, and James Bailey.

A second group who have earned our lasting gratitude is the staff of the Loma Linda University library, La Sierra Campus, for their gracious assistance in the constant search for authoritative published materials. We especially thank two staff members, Grace Holm and Shirley Eagler, for their reading of the manuscript in its early stages.

A third group, most of whom were students of Loma Linda University, cheerfully adjusted their schedules to do our typing and retyping.

Preface

A Vegetarian Diet is a book about vegetarians and vegetarianism. Its authors are vegetarians of many years' standing and experience. Nevertheless, the purpose of the book is not to convert the nonvegetarian to a meatless lifestyle. A number of books directed toward that goal are already available. The purpose is primarily to help those who have already made, or are making, the change to vegetarianism as they search for increased health and greater satisfaction. Secondarily, its purpose is to answer the many questions of the family and friends of vegetarians about the why, and particularly the how, of this (to them) new way of life. It is intended to make clear the difference between genuine vegetarianism and pseudovegetarianism.

It also emphasizes the essential difference in the two common forms of vegetarianism—the lacto-ovo and total vegetarian types.

The book is not to be used as a therapeutic tool. A meatless diet, no matter how healthful and satisfying otherwise, and no matter how scientifically planned, is not a substitute for medical diagnosis and care. Indeed, many diseases affect the digestion, absorption, or metabolism of foods to the extent that drastic changes in eating patterns must be made. People with health problems who attempt to treat themselves with diet alone, ignoring capable health practitioners, are not merely asking for trouble, they are demanding it. This book is not for them.

A third purpose of the book is to combat the unfavorable publicity which, even today, the vegetarian way of eating sometimes receives. Many well-meaning critics have simply never met in person this delightful way of life. It is unfortunate that the vegetarian system has so often been negatively caricatured. This book attempts to picture vegetarianism as it really is at its best—abounding in health-promoting nutrients, aglow with color, excellent in texture and flavor, and uncontaminated by animal suffering and death.

Chapter 1

A Vegetarian Diet: What It Is; What It Is Not

In every age and in many lands, vegetarianism has been adopted by a few devoted and determined individuals, while ridiculed with equal zest by others. However, this practice, once followed only by a few religious and philosophical groups, is now fairly common and has become widely known, if not well understood.

First, what is vegetarianism? How do vegetarians differ from nonvegetarians? How do they obtain sufficient nutritional essentials? Do they enjoy their meals and have good health, or are they willing but deprived sufferers for a mistaken and valueless cause? Are they food faddists? Are they quacks?

Second, why do they conduct their lives in this restricted fashion? Why do they maintain an eating style which goes

13

contrary to almost every popular concept of pleasurable dining in this and most historical time periods? Why do they disdain an entire category of well-known foods in favor of less esteemed dishes? Answers to these and other questions are the purpose of this book.

What Is A Vegetarian Diet?

It is sometimes stated that a vegetarian diet, by definition, must involve complete abstinence from all animal products, including milk, cheese, and eggs. Although this concept is logical, many people who consider themselves vegetarians do use some or all of these products. Therefore, a distinction has developed between flesh products (meat, fish, poultry) and nonflesh animal products (milk, cheese, eggs, etc.).

Three main types, or levels, of vegetarianism are commonly recognized: lacto-ovo-, lacto *or* ovo, and total vegetarianism. Lacto-ovo-vegetarians use nonflesh animal products. The lacto- or ovo-vegetarians limit these products to dairy foods or eggs but do not include both. The Trappist monks, for example, are said to be a lacto group, using some milk and cheese but no eggs.[1] Pure, or total vegetarians, sometimes called vegans, use no egg or dairy products. Their diet consists of fruits and vegetables, legumes, nuts, and grains. Traditional and some modern vegan groups will not use even nonfood animal products such as leather, wool, fur, or feathers.

Many knowledgeable persons, however, believe that vegetarians eat fish and other seafoods. This assumption may be due in part to the frequent association of vegetarianism with religious customs. Until recent years many Christians abstained from red meat, but not from fish, on Fridays. According to one authoritative source, some so-called vegetarians do consume fish.[2] This is not a generally accepted definition by vegetarians themselves.

The *World Book Encyclopedia* follows the usual terminology by defining vegetarianism as the custom of living on a meatless diet, with both fish and fowl classified as meat.[3] The *Encyclopaedia Britannica* defines a vegetarian as an abstainer from all flesh products. He may or may not also abstain from eggs and dairy products.[4] *The Random House Dictionary* describes the vegetarian as a nonconsumer of flesh products whether meat, fish, or fowl, and sometimes of any animal food product whatsoever. The practice may be based on either nutritional or ethical standards.[5]

Earlier works may use a more restricted definition than later ones, thereby pointing up the recent increase in information about this way of life. Thus, *Webster's Collegiate Dictionary*, 1971, used the plant-products-only definition,[6] but the 1973 edition includes animal, i.e., dairy products.[7]

But there are dietary regimens going far beyond the vegetarian system. There are fruitarians who live mainly on fruits and nuts, and others who consume only raw foods. One medical dictionary is quoted as defining a strict vegetarian as one excluding from his diet plant foods other than those grown above the ground in the sunlight.[8] The very popular zen macrobiotic diet of the sixties was presented to many young Americans as a series of ten progressively restricted eating patterns. The lowest did not differ much from what many of these people were accustomed to receiving at home. As the ten-rung ladder of deletions continued upward, animal foods were quickly eliminated. However, before these animal products were dropped altogether, fruits were withdrawn. Salads were taboo, as were certain vegetables. In its extreme form—the tenth and top rung—the diet consisted only of natural cereals and a few seasonings. Even liquids, including water, were drastically curtailed.[9]

Followers of all of these programs are often referred to as vegetarians, but these practices go far beyond vegetarianism. The vegetarian diet may include all common edible kinds of plant life, fruits, vegetables, legumes, nuts, grains. Lacto-ovo-vegetarians use, in addition, dairy products and eggs.

Vegetarianism is not the same as the natural foods movement. Neither is it the same as the organic foods movement. It differs from both of these systems in its concentration on one factor—a diet composed largely of plant foods and excluding all flesh products. Undoubtedly some vegetarians prefer those foods defined as organically grown, just as many of them use generous quantities of raw fruits and vegetables. Many use whole-grain breads and cereals in preference to the refined products. Probably most vegetarians regard their eating pattern as the prime example of "natural" food habits. But the basic distinction separating vegetarianism from main-line American food customs remains simply the exclusion of flesh food products.

Is A Vegetarian Diet Nutritionally Sound?

The most important question to ask about any dietary system is whether it is adequate. The vegetarian diet is indeed adequate. In fact, because it requires a large variety of fruits and vegetables with their store of minerals and vitamins and high fiber content, it actually surpasses some less varied nonvegetarian meal plans.

Certain cautions are, of course, in order, especially for the beginning vegetarian. Everyone needs a practical knowledge of nutrition, the vegetarian no less than his meat-eating friends and neighbors.

The mere fact of omitting meat, fish, and poultry will not make a diet inadequate. If it is initially inadequate, or if, in the process of adopting a vegetarian diet, too many foods are left out, then of course problems will follow. The new vegetarian must be sufficiently aware of nutritional requirements to obtain all of his needs. Otherwise his careful choice of diet may backfire and he may suffer from a lack of some nutrient which he previously might have obtained by accident.

Fortunately, nutritional adequacy is not at all difficult for the vegetarian. In terms of nutrition, lacto-ovo diets are very similar to a diet including meat. If otherwise balanced, they are entirely adequate to sustain excellent health. They often excel in some nutrients, such as calcium.

The total vegetarian, however, must find and use alternate sources of one or more missing nutrients. For this reason, many lacto-ovo-vegetarians are strongly opposed to a total vegetarian diet. They fear a predisposition to malnutrition through unmet needs for vitamin B_{12} and vitamin D, along with possible short supplies of some minerals. In a generally affluent nation whose cultural food heritage includes much emphasis upon animal products, these dangers are real. They need not, however, pose problems. The total vegetarian way of eating certainly requires more care, but can be maintained safely, provided the eater himself understands the system and follows it wisely. In May 1974, the Food and Nutrition Board of the National Research Council, a branch of the National Academy of Sciences, published a statement affirming the safety of the vegetarian regimen when carefully prepared to include all essential nutrients. This statement discusses the hazards of the most restricted level, the total vegetarian diet, and includes suggestions for ensuring adequacy.[10]

The vegetarian way of life is completely safe as long as all meal patterns meet the standard of scientific principles of nutrition. And this standard is in no way difficult to reach.

Information vs. Misinformation

It is entirely possible for a vegetarian, or a meat eater for that matter, to be a faddist. Food faddism involves belief, without any scientifically demonstrable basis, in the protective or curative properties of certain products. Or it may have to do with entirely unproved benefits of abstinence from other products. There are many examples in nutrition history and many more in existence today. Some reducing diets are notorious cases. Consumption of large quantities of specialized food products, e.g., wheat germ, black-strap molasses, etc., can become another form of faddism. Many of these products are both useful and delectable; the faddism occurs when their use is carried to excess and when great, but untested, claims are made as to their benefits.

Of course, we should not classify everything with which we do not immediately agree as faddism. Occasionally some previously unfounded claim is discovered through later research to have a scientific basis. The knowledgeable person, however, will not carry even a good idea to excess, and he will be perceptive enough to discern the difference between well-founded nutritional information and what may be merely glib statements without any factual basis.

So far as we know, no research has ever been attempted to determine whether the vegetarian or the nonvegetarian is more likely to be a "food faddist." There appears to be no question, however, that the vegetarian is more likely to be accused of food faddism. Occasionally, although rarely, a current writer actually classifies vegetarianism with faddism. This attitude is clearly a hangover from the past. There are at least three reasons for its occurrence:

1. Vegetarianism is still not widely accepted as a way of life for the affluent majority. Quite naturally, the small group which varies from prevailing customs is considered the deviant group.

2. Within the limits of historical acceptance, vegetarianism has existed for many, many centuries. During the years of prescientific views and practices, vegetarians obviously could not give a very scientific account of themselves. Neither could nonvegetarians, for that matter, but they were the majority and did not have to justify their customs.

3. More recently, vegetarianism has become associated in the minds of many persons with extremist practices. It will take time to separate these groups in popular thinking.

In the meantime, acquisition of basic nutritional knowledge, plus the development of good food habits, will raise the status of the individual vegetarian safely above accusations of faddism.

Now, to go a step further, may vegetarianism in any way, directly or indirectly, be associated with quackery? Certainly not vegetarianism as we view it. *The Random House Dictionary* defines a quack as someone professing to possess qualifications which he does not have.[11]

In years gone by, before the advent of experimental nutrition research in the United States, many claims were made for dietary regimens on the basis of personal experience, superstition, fantasy, etc. Vegetarians were not alone, nor peculiar, in making these claims. For example, writers in the *Dietetic and Hygienic Gazette,* published about 1900, made many stout claims on both sides of the argument. One hopeful physician published his belief that merely increased use of raw plant foods would solve the entire problem of cancer.[12] In earlier issues that same year two physicians had expressed their belief that beef consumption helped to prevent leprosy[13] and that swordfish and soft clams would greatly benefit the insane. Shellfish would cure dyspepsia, and salt pork was especially nourishing for miners.[14]

Today, sufficient evidence from experimental and statistical research has made it unnecessary to concoct fanciful tales of health and healing to justify choice of a nonmeat dietary. The modern speaker or writer who refers to vegetarian habits as quackery often has confused vegetarianism with a more extreme system.

Vegetarian Lifestyles

Once the adequacy of a vegetarian diet is established, other questions may arise. Are good eating habits difficult to maintain? Is the system synonomous with deprivation?

Vegetarianism is many things to many people. Generally, it is one aspect of a total way of life. And this way of life may differ somewhat from one committed group to another, one culture to another, one period of time to another. All vegetarians the world around, or even in one culture, cannot be classified under one heading.

In the long run this movement, like most others, will be judged by the success, i.e., the health and social standing, of its adherents. If ordinary, everyday, sensible people, the people who make good neighbors and good friends, are observed living happy, healthy, productive lives on a vegetarian regimen, then the vegetarian diet will be accepted, though not necessarily followed, by the majority of people. How does it stand up to such a challenge today?

Judging by numerous references in current nutrition literature, many people believe that life is somehow more difficult for nonmeat eaters. Vegetarians are seen as having to work harder, chew more energetically, and generally exert themselves to an unreasonable and unwarranted degree to obtain their protein from the plant world. All this could be avoided, of course, by utilizing the high-quality protein resources generously provided by nature and the livestock, fish, poultry, and dairy industries.

It is true that animal protein, with the exception of gelatin, is of high biological value and the amount per unit of meat, milk, and eggs is usually fairly large. Plant protein is generally of lower biological value and often less concentrated in terms of quantity. But it is an oversimplification to assert that animal protein is therefore first-class material and plant protein second class. Both must be broken down into their building components, the amino acids, before being used by the body. Meanwhile, vegetarians enjoy strawberries, granola, lentils, spinach and pecan patties with as much relish as the consumers of T-bone steak and shrimp salad enjoy the foods of their preference.

Perhaps the most widespread of all misconceptions about this mode of life is that it involves deprivation. Traditionally, in many parts of the world, subsistence on plant food has been associated with extreme poverty. Even today, for many in the poorer areas of the world, deprivation is a fact of life, not from choice but from the harsh conditions of economic and technological underdevelopment.

Years ago, before the birth of the life sciences as we know them today, people selected foods largely on the basis of obtainability. In his *History of Nutrition,* Elmer McCollum showed how, during most of human history and over most of the globe, availability rather than concern for nutritive quality determined eating habits. And this availability depended upon location, climate, and such geographic resources as water to provide fish, woodlands with their wild game, or fertile areas with an abundance of plant life. Thus some races were dependent upon animal and others upon vegetable foods.[15]

But within a given area food supplies often depended, as they do today, upon each family's place on the broad and uneven scales of wealth and poverty. The well-to-do inhabitants of the castle fortress consumed course after spicy course of roast meat, roast fowl, and roast fish. The poor laborer and his family outside the walls gnawed their heavy peasant bread with its pitiful accompaniment of scanty herbs. At least this is the popular picture which has come down to us. Certainly, wealth provided resources which the poor were denied. All the abilities of skilled cooks, some of whom were persons of considerable prominence in the homes of their high-placed employers, were combined with the available range of animals, birds, and fish to support feasting and the good life. Even the middle-class urban gentleman might enjoy two or three kinds of meat dishes—but with few or no vegetables, which were left to the more "deprived" classes.

Many dedicated followers of the world's great religions courageously embraced rigid systems of asceticism, and flesh foods were among the first and most widespread prohibitions. From the early days of the Christian church large numbers of devout persons observed periods of fasting, and entire monastic groups lived out their lives on meatless dietaries. Thus, in the minds of many of America's forebears, a vegetarian diet was associated with poverty and an ascetic life, sort of a last sorrowful word in individual and community deprivation. In contrast, flesh foods were the stuff of which came feasts and gladness of heart.

But intelligent vegetarianism today denies this traditional concept. It effectively negates the assertion that, since meat has long been the food of the prosperous, meat is therefore of all foods most desirable. In the fascinating history of men's food and feasting, there is an infinity of difference between the serf's coarse black bread and limited supply of "herbs" and the sophisticated array of artistically combined colors, delicate flavors, and varied textures of a modern vegetarian buffet. More than one astonished diner has come away from such a meal declaring, "If this is vegetarianism, I can accept it."

True vegetarianism, when it becomes a way of life through free choice and knowledgeable planning, can offer as delicious and delectable a pattern as can the use of the most expensive animal foods. It is not deprivation; it is not hardship. Its followers are not quacks; they are not faddists; they are not malnourished. Meatless mealtimes are currently the chosen way of life of many happy and healthy consumers.

References

1. *Encyclopaedia Britannica* (1971), s.v. "Cistercians."

2. Caleb W. David, "Vegetarianism," *Collier's Encyclopedia* (1975), pp. 58-59.

3. Willard Jacobson, "Vegetarianism," *World Book Encyclopedia* (1973), p. 236.

4. *Encyclopaedia Britannica* (1971), s.v. "Vegetarianism."

5. *The Random House Dictionary of the English Language*, unabridged ed., (1973), s.v. "vegetarian."

6. *Webster's Seventh New Collegiate Dictionary*, based on *Webster's Third International Dictionary* (1971), s.v. "vegetarian."

7. *Webster's New Collegiate Dictionary* (1973), s.v. "vegetarian."

8. *Stedman's Medical Dictionary*, 21st ed. (1966). Quoted in *Vegetarianism*, by R. A. Seelig (Washington: United Fresh Fruit and Vegetable Association, March 1976).

9. S. Nyoiti, *You Are All Sanpaku*, English version by William Dufty (New York: University Books, 1965).

10. *Vegetarian Diets*, A Statement of the Food and Nutrition Board, Division of Biological Sciences, Assembly of Life Sciences, National Research Council (Washington: National Academy of Sciences, May 1974).

11. *The Random House Dictionary of the English Language*, s.v. "quack."

12. Robert Bell, "The Dietetics of Cancer," *The Dietetic and Hygienic Gazette* (December 1906), pp. 705–11.

13. Ephraim Cutter and John Asburton Cutter, "Food: Its Relation to Health and Disease," *The Dietetic and Hygienic Gazette* (March 1906), pp. 151-56.

14. Ibid., (June 1906), pp. 340-48.

15. Elmer Verner McCollum, *A History of Nutrition* (Boston: Houghton, Mifflin, 1957), p. 1.

Chapter 2

Filet Mignon
or Pecan Patties

When Mr. and Mrs. Average Person learn that their children are becoming vegetarians, their first verbal reaction may be, "But where are they going to get enough protein?"

Knowledge of this body-building substance began with early scientific research approximately 150 years ago. At that time Gerardus Mulder, a Dutch chemist, named it *protein*, from a Greek word meaning "to take first place." Much later scientists discovered that protein was made up of a number of individual units which they named amino acids, and that proteins from different sources were composed of different combinations of these amino acids.

Composition of Proteins

Protein, like carbohydrate and fat, contains three common elements of the physical world: carbon, hydrogen, and oxygen. But it also contains a fourth element distinguishing it from the other energy sources—nitrogen. And it is principally nitrogen which gives protein, in the form of its individual amino acids, the unique ability to produce new tissues and to repair worn tissues. Of course, without its accompanying vitamins and minerals and the constant supply of energy, even protein would be useless as a body builder.

Some amino acids can be made by the human body itself, provided the materials are supplied by food. Others cannot be synthesized by humans, and these must be furnished ready-made in the food. Those which must be supplied in the food are known as "essential" amino acids, and the others, which the body can make, "nonessential." However, the nonessential units are quite as essential, in the sense of being required, as the essential amino acids which must come from the food we eat.

Eight of these essential units are required by adults in their food: isoleucine, leucine, lysine, methionine, phenylalanine, threonine, tryptophan, and valine. A ninth, histidine, has been considered as essential for small children, but some recent evidence indicates that histidine may be needed by adults as well.[1]

The nonessential amino acids, which, given the materials, the healthy body can synthesize for itself, include: alanine, arginine, aspartic acid, citrulline, cystine, glutamic acid, glycine, hydroxyproline, proline, serine, and tyrosine.

A protein containing sufficient quantities of all of the essential amino acids, those which the human body cannot synthesize, is considered *complete* and of *high biological value.* If one or more of these essential amino acids is low or missing altogether, the protein is incomplete.

For many years it was generally thought that everyone must use as many complete proteins as possible to assure a good diet. This meant using animal proteins, since these substances—with the exception of gelatin—contain all the essential amino acids in proportions similar to those found in humans. Thus meat, milk, and eggs came to be regarded by many persons as first-class proteins. Plant proteins, which generally lack adequate amounts of one or more essential amino acids, were correspondingly labeled second class, or even lower, on the nutritive scale. Such a distinction is somewhat superficial. Ultimate biological value must be assessed, not on individual proteins, but on the total amino acids of all these proteins included in the meal. It is the total which the body will use, and this total may be considerably higher than the level in any one of the individual proteins.

In the United States a chemical score has been developed, using whole egg protein as a standard, i.e., 100 percent, by which to evaluate the biological value of a protein for meal planning or feeding purposes. This evaluation predicts how completely the protein will meet the needs of the human (or other organism) to be fed. Foods and food combinations of high biological value will meet the following needs:

1. Development of new tissues as in pregnancy, growth, restoration of tissue destroyed by burns or other trauma, and muscular development.

2. Daily maintenance and repair of normal tissue with its more or less constant wear and tear.

Protein foods and food combinations of low biological value may be able to handle some—not all—of the daily repair tasks but fail to provide for needed new tissues.

Moreover, predicted values based on the chemical score are not always realized. The first problem is digestibility. If a food contains considerable indigestible matter—not necessarily a disadvantage—the protein, regardless of its natural biological value, will be reduced in availability.

Second is the occurrence of the *Browning*, or *Maillard*, reaction in some products. This change, called either Browning after the alteration in color, or Maillard after the name of the person first identifying it, results from heavy heating of the amino acid lysine in combination with certain carbohydrates in the same food. This heating brings about a tight chemical bond which human digestive enzymes cannot break down. Lysine, one of the essential amino acids, thus becomes unavailable. Heavy toasting, as of some cereals, is one example.[2]

Protein Quality and Meal Patterns

Many persons believe that the total vegetarian must supplement plant proteins at every meal. The rice and beans, or the oats and peanuts, or the sesame and garbanzos must be eaten together or their supplementary value will be lost. This concept is based on animal research which has demonstrated the timing of amino acid combinations to be vital.

Animals used in such research undergo strict nutritional limitations. These limitations seldom prevail in human adult dietaries based on free choice and adequate resources. It is true that one essential amino acid cannot be stored to await the arrival of its missing mates before proceeding with the formation of new protein in the cells.[3] The objective of combining protein foods to produce a high-quality mixture at each meal is in line with this concept.

But most whole grains and legumes contain at least small amounts of the essential amino acids, although grains are low in lysine and legumes in methionine. Moreover, the continuous normal, healthy breakdown of body cells adds a temporary supply of amino acids to the body pool. Thus, the vegetarian who daily consumes an adequate quantity and quality of plant protein, and who does not lack sufficient sources of energy or other protein-related requirements, is unlikely to suffer damage as a result of a low specific amino acid intake in one meal. Persons regularly consuming very low amounts of protein, whether for reasons of economy, weight reduction, or overly restricted (pseudo-vegetarianism) patterns, could be at considerable risk.

How Much Protein Is Needed?

A frequent question among both vegetarians and meat eaters is: How much protein should the average adult eat daily? From the early years of protein research to the present the recommendations for Americans have decreased considerably in amount. Some early estimates were based on the diets of healthy working men. Meat was plentiful and popular. Other foods such as cereals were consumed to the extent that even their low protein levels raised the total intake. In 1881 in Germany, Carl Voit determined that 118 grams daily was a reasonable amount for a moderately active male,[4] and this estimate was at first accepted in the United States. W. A. Atwater, of the U. S. Department of Agriculture, was one of the first Americans to engage in scientific research in foods and nutrition. After studying in Germany, he returned to the United States and devoted much time to research in the nutritional values of American foods. He recommended consumption of 125 grams of protein daily for American men.[5]

Additional surveys of the foods men selected for their own consumption caused the scientists to raise these recommendations. Finally, by 1900 Voit was advocating 145 grams, and Atwater and Max Rubner, a professor of physiology in a German university, 150 grams.[6]

Then very early in the 1900s the downward trend began. R. H. Chittenden, a Yale University professor, experimented with a greatly reduced protein intake. After using himself as a subject and becoming convinced that his own health had improved, he began experimenting with Yale students. Thereafter he recommended a protein level revised to approximately one-half of Voit's initial recommendation.[7]

At about the same time considerable publicity was given to comparative endurance records of vegetarians and non-vegetarians. To the puzzlement of many, vegetarians seemed to come off victorious. Then the subject was dropped. Nutrition research was about to enter an era of rapid expansion, and fascinating discoveries were just around the corner. One of the first surprises in store was the news that not all proteins possessed the same biological value.[8] Henceforth there were to be complete proteins (meat, milk, and egg) and incomplete proteins (cereal and vegetable). A decade later the emergence of mysterious substances to be called first *vitamines* and later *vitamins* was about to begin. In the meantime more and more became known about those amazing bits of inorganic matter, the minerals.

The vegetarian way of life was almost a lost cause except to a few die-hard enthusiasts. But not again would recommended protein levels soar to the heights proposed by Voit, Atwater, and Rubner. These men made contributions of great worth to the health of mankind. They had large shares in the difficult task of establishing nutrition as a world science. They could not, with the research tools available to them in their day, and in line with the concepts of their time, accomplish today's scientific marvels.

By the mid-twentieth century the recommended daily allowance (RDA) for protein seemed satisfactory to just about everyone. Seventy grams was considered a safe allowance for the average man, 65 grams for the average woman. "Average" referred to size and activity. Age was in a different category, with young growing bodies requiring more protein per unit of body weight. And, of course, pregnancy and breast feeding increased a woman's requirement.

Table 1. *Protein Values of Selected Foods*

Food	*Amount*	*Grams of protein*
Bread	1 slice	2
Cereal, cooked	½–1 cup	1½–5*
Cereal, ready to eat	½–1 cup	1–5*
Macaroni, noodles, spaghetti, cooked	1 cup	4–6½
Miscellaneous fruits	average serving	½
Miscellaneous vegetables, cooked	½–1 cup	1–2
Green peas, cooked	½ cup	4
Green lima beans, cooked	½ cup	6
Legumes (dried peas, beans, etc.) cooked	½ cup	6–7
Peanuts, roasted	1 tablespoon	4
Peanut butter	1 tablespoon	4
Cashew nuts	6–8 nuts	2½
Brazil nuts	2 medium nuts	1
Cheese, cheddar	1 ounce	7
Eggs	1	6
Milk	8 ounces	8
Meat analogs		Variable: see individual package label

Source: Adapted from *Nutritive Value of American Foods in Common Units*, Agricultural Handbook No. 456 (Washington, D.C.: Agricultural Research Service, U.S. Department of Agriculture, 1975).

*Some brands are higher in protein than others. Two grams per half-cup cooked cereal is a commonly used figure. Many ready-to-eat cereals list their protein values on the package labels.

But in 1973, RDA figures were decreased to 56 grams for men and 46 for women. These amounts were based on (1) nitrogen balance (intake vs. output) studies, (2) 30 percent addition to cover individual variation in needs, and (3) another addition to cover normal inefficiency in the actual utilization of protein in the body.[9] The end result was 0.8 of a gram per kilogram (2.2 pounds) of body weight, or 56 grams for a man of average size and normal weight (approximately 154 pounds).

A few persons assert that these figures are too low. Most authorities regard them as entirely safe. In our view, the 56- and 46- gram figures allow a margin of safety for individual conditions and variations. Certainly the RDA figures are not difficult to reach, as the approximate protein values in Table 1 indicate.

Many, probably most, Americans obtain considerably more than the recommended allowances. Groups at risk, those whose protein intakes may be inadequate, generally are the same ones whose meals are unbalanced in other nutritional factors. They are usually low in mineral and vitamin consumption. The elderly, the very poor, those with serious diet problems, those with poor food habits, and the few who follow bizarre diet practices for reducing or other purposes, are often lacking in protective foods. Insufficient protein is one phase of the total problem.

To assure an adequate diet the vegetarian, like the meat eater, must use a variety of nutritious foods. This may actually be easier for the vegetarian, who depends upon several foods instead of one for much of his nourishment. Naturally, all of the kinds of foods should not be included in the same meal, although some sources of protein and most of the other nutrients should be there.

Supplementation of Plant Protein

If only natural plant proteins are used, the need for supplementation dictates that cereals should be used during the day in one or more of the following combinations:

1. Other cereals with supplementary amino acid patterns, legumes, nuts, or leafy green vegetables. Examples include corn or rice with beans.[10]

2. Soy combined (as in soy-whole wheat bread) with wheat, corn, or rye.

3. Cereals (including breads) with legumes and green leafy vegetables.

Two Kinds of Vegetarian Diet

All the nutritional values of the "four food groups" may be found in a well planned vegetarian diet. Above is shown a nutritionally complete assortment of pure vegetarian ("vegan") foods with protein-rich foods at the left including commercial meat substitutes and fortified soymilk as well as purely "natural" protein foods such as soy products, legumes, grains, and nuts. Even the green, leafy vegetables contain protein as well as vitamins and minerals—to be found also in a generous variety of other fruits and vegetables. Below is a lacto-ovo-vegetarian assortment, including eggs and dairy products.

"The vegetarian diet is indeed adequate. In fact, because it requires a large variety of fruits and vegetables with their store of minerals and vitamins and high fiber content it actually surpasses some less varied nonvegetarian meal plans."

"*A balanced meal pattern should be high in natural foods — whole grain breads and cereals, fruits and vegetables; it should contain a wide variety of foods; it should be free of 'empty calories,' foods that are largely without minerals, vitamins, or proteins.*"

Nature's Harvest

4. Peanuts with wheat, oats, corn, or rice.

5. Garbanzos and sesame.

A combination of soy and sesame proteins is said to be comparable to the protein of milk.[11]

Remember, these foods must be in their unrefined state; refined cereals, flours, and breads would be unlikely to yield the same results.

People in different parts of the world have maintained adequate protein nutrition by such combinations, which soon become second nature to cook and eater alike. The Chinese have used the cereal combination method to obtain protein of good quality.[12] They also emphasize green leafy vegetables. These green leafy vegetables, generally low only in methionine among the essential amino acids, are widely used in many parts of the world. Corn or rice, with certain legumes, are also used in areas without adequate animal resources. However, where meat is plentiful and popular, most persons will probably ignore these combinations, or use them only as accompaniments.

Table 2. *Supplementary Plant Proteins*

Corn or rice	with	Beans
Bread or cereal	with	Legumes
Peanuts	with	Wheat, oats, corn, or rice
Garbanzos	with	Sesame seeds
Soy	with	Sesame seeds
Soy flour	with	Wheat, corn or rye

A number of innovative food processors have developed canned and frozen meat alternates, often called meat analogs, for use in vegetarian meals. Some of these products meet vegan diet standards; others contain small amounts of albumen or other nonplant products. Although much more research needs to be done on these alternates, the composition of many would appear to assure their users of good protein value. Some of them are suitable for use in entrees, some in sandwiches, some as milk substitutes. Many are fortified with certain minerals and vitamins common in meat products. Perhaps their chief current disadvantage is their cost. However, the cost is often not above that of comparable meat products.

Is There Danger of Too Much Protein?

Can healthy persons consume too much protein? This is an area begging for more research. Was the superiority of the vegetarians participating in endurance tests due to their lower protein intake or to dietaries containing higher levels of vitamins and other nutrients unknown to the science of the early 1900s?

We continue to hear today about the vegetarian athletes who establish new records, and also about the old-fashioned believers in the athlete's need for good red meat and plenty of it. It is known that carbohydrate for energy is vital and that more water is required to utilize protein than for either carbohydrate or fat.[13] Much more research is needed for an understanding of endurance trends in relation to diet.

The same is true of questions regarding potential damage caused by a high-protein diet. Such questions extend far beyond the generally recognized hazards of certain types of protein foods such as high-fat meats. In the early 1900s Chittenden's research began to point out the adequacy of an intake of protein much lower than had previously been recommended. Chittenden himself was convinced that the lower level was beneficial and that there was some danger in an excess of protein.[14]

There are reports from animal research of enlarged kidneys believed to be due to elimination of excess protein end-products.[15] One physician believes that the same excess affects human beings in the same way.[16] There are reports that a high protein intake results in higher losses from the body of some other nutrients, including calcium.[17] Other writers call attention to the great variation in protein intake among healthy human adults with no evidence of damage.[18] Children, however, are reported to be sensitive to intakes considerably in excess of need.[19]

Final answers to the question must await further research. In the meantime the vegetarian has placed a voluntary curb on his own intake. For, although it is entirely possible for lacto-ovo-vegetarians to eat huge quantities of protein foods—eggs, dairy products, legumes, meat analogs—they are less likely to do so than persons with a high consumption of meats and dairy foods. Costs and calories may well enter into the personal solution also. The vegetarian enjoys—or soon learns to enjoy—a variety of fruits and vegetables, some of which are relatively low in both calories and costs, at least when compared with some protein foods.

Vitamin B$_{12}$

Because of its availability in animal products vitamin B_{12} might be said to be related to protein. The vitamin is produced by microorganisms in the soil, in chlorella algae and some sea algae. In spite of diligent search no land plant source with any significant amount of vitamin B_{12} activity has been discovered. Animals, who harbor the organisms, transmit the vitamin to humans in meat, milk, and eggs. The total vegetarian obtains some from fortified meat analogs and fortified soy milks. It is added to some prepared cereals.

Before the discovery of this vitamin in 1948, pernicious anemia was a crippling and fatal disease, with only one successful treatment—eating large quantities of liver or receiving injections of liver extract. Before the vitamin itself was isolated from liver, researchers had learned that without a specific gastrointestinal factor pernicious anemia could develop. Requirements therefore included both the stomach's digestive enzymes and an external substance coming into the body through the food supply. In 1948, this second factor became known as vitamin B_{12}. It was first isolated in the amount of one gram (a penny weighs approximately five grams) from four tons of animal livers.[20]

Many total vegetarians have developed lesions symptomatic of vitamin B_{12} deficiency. These lesions involve damage to the myelin tissue of the central nervous system, ultimately crippling the victim. This nerve damage is prevented by vitamin B_{12}. Persons with slight damage may complain of tingling sensations in hands and feet. The anemia accompanying these lesions often responds to treatment with folic acid, another B vitamin. Folic acid, however, will provide no help for the nerve damage.

Some adult vegans in the United States have been able to maintain health for years with no known source of vitamin B_{12}. A currently accepted theory is that much of the vitamin is secreted in the bile and reabsorbed low in the intestinal tract, and recycled to the body tissues.[21] This recycling of the vitamin would, of course, be dependent upon adequate stores to begin with. Children would be at grave risk. Occasionally hope has been held out that under optimum conditions human beings, like animals, could obtain their own vitamin B_{12} from bacterial synthesis in the intestinal tract. Until proof of such synthesis is obtained, total vegetarians, especially children, adolescents, and pregnant women, must have some outside dependable source of the vitamin.

Minerals and Vitamins

In addition to protein and vitamin B_{12}, many nutrition authorities list calcium, iron, and riboflavin among the nutrients that may be limited in a total vegetarian diet. Milk is an important source of calcium and riboflavin. In addition, its protein is of high quality; it supplies sufficient vitamin B$_{12}$ for child and adult; whole milk is a good source of vitamin A; and most fluid milks are vitamin D fortified. It is easy to see why milk occupies such a large place in American eating habits. To replace it in the diet requires attention to a half dozen vital nutrients.

Calcium and riboflavin can be obtained, in fairly generous amounts, from other sources. Both are found in most dark green leafy vegetables; riboflavin is contained also in whole grain or enriched cereals and breads. The calcium content of these vegetables, and that of other sources, is less than the amount obtained from generous supplies of milk. This appears not to be a problem, however, on well-balanced diets.[22]

Iron falls below the recommended daily amount in the diet of many Americans, especially women and girls of childbearing age. This is true for meat eaters as well as nonmeat eaters. It may well be that in this instance the total vegetarian actually fares best of all, because of his generally high intake of legumes, nuts, dark green leafy vegetables, and dried fruits.

Thus, it is an established fact today that the vegetarian diet can well supply both the quantity and quality of protein and the few nutrients, about which concern is often expressed: calcium, riboflavin, iron, and—with the help of fortified foods and/or a vitamin supplement for the total vegetarian—vitamin B$_{12}$.

Mr. and Mrs. Average Person can be assured that their vegetarian children will get the nutrients they need so long as they pay attention to their total diet. Dinner may be pecan patties rather than filet mignon, but it will be nourishing— and less expensive.

References

1. J. D. Kopple and M. E. S. Swendseid, *Evidence for a Dietary Histidine Requirement in Normal Man*, (Abstr.), Fed. Proc. 331: 691 (1974). Cited by Jean Weininger and George M. Briggs, "Nutrition Update, 1974," *Journal of Nutrition Education* 6 (October-December 1974): 139-43.

2. Aaron M. Altschul, *Proteins, Their Chemistry and Politics* (New York: Basic Books, 1965), p. 154.

3. Ibid., p. 118.

4. Ibid., p. 96. See also Elmer Verner McCollum, *A History of Nutrition*, (Boston: Houghton, Mifflin, 1957), pp. 191-92.

5. McCollum, p. 192.

6. Ibid.

7. Ibid., pp. 193-95, 196.

8. Ibid., pp. 197-99.

9. National Research Council. Food and Nutrition Board. Committee on Dietary Allowances. Committee on Interpretation of the Recommended Dietary Allowances, *Recommended Dietary Allowances*, 8th rev. ed. (Washington: National Academy of Sciences, 1974), p. 47.

10. A. Sanchez, J. A. Sharffenberg, and U. D. Register, "Nutrition Values of Selected Proteins and Protein Combinations. I. The Biological Value of Proteins Singly and in Meal Patterns with Varying Fat Composition," *American Journal of Clinical Nutrition* 13 (1963): 243.

11. M. Narayana Rao and M. Swaminathan, "Plant Proteins in the Amelioration of Protein Deficiency States," in *World Review of Nutrition and Dietetics*, vol. 11, ed. Geoffrey H. Bourne (Basel, Switzerland and New York: S. Karger, 1969), pp. 106-41.

12. Anthony A. Albanese and Louise A. Orto, "The Proteins and Amino Acids," in *Modern Nutrition in Health and Disease*, ed. Robert S. Goodhart and Maurice E. Shils, 5th ed. (Philadelphia: Lea and Febiger, 1973), pp. 28-88.

13. Ibid.

14. Sir Stanley Davidson, R. Passmore, J. F. Brock, and A. S. Truswell, *Human Nutrition and Dietetics*, 6th ed. (Edinburgh: Churchill Livingstone, Medical Division of Longman Group Ltd., 1975), p. 68.

15. E. Schilling, "Effect of Excess Protein Feeding for Several Years on the Structure of the Bovine Kidney," *Nutritional Abstracts and Reviews* 33 (1963):114; T. B. Osborne, L. B. Mendel, E. A. Park, and M. C. Winternitz, "Physiological Effects of Diet Unusually Rich in Protein or Inorganic Salts," *Journal of Biological Chemistry* 71 (1926-27):317-50.

16. L. Emmett Holt, "Nutrition in a Changing World, Perspectives in Nutrition," *American Journal of Clinical Nutrition* 11 (November 1962): 543-48.

17. Nancy E. Johnson, Emerita N. Alcantara and Helen Linkswiler, "Effect of Level of Protein Intake on Urinary and Fecal Calcium and Calcium Retention of Young Adult Males," *Journal of Nutrition* 100 (De-

cember 1970): 1425-30;S. Margen, J. Y. Chu, N. A. Kaufman, and D. H. Calloway, "Studies in Calcium Metabolism. I. The Calciuretic Effect of Dietary Protein," *American Journal of Clinical Nutrition* 27 (June 1974):584-89; and M. Rechcigl, Jr., S. Berger, J. K. Loosli, and H. H. Williams, "Dietary Protein and Utilization of Vitamin A," *Journal of Nutrition* 76 (April 1962):435-40; O. A. Roels, "Vitamin A Physiology," *Journal of the American Medical Association* 214 (November 1970):1097-1102.

18. Davidson et al, *Human Nutrition*, pp. 68, 69.

19. Albanese and Orto, "Proteins and Amino Acids," pp. 28-88.

20. "Further Studies on Vitamin B12," *Nutrition Reviews* 6 (October 1948):291-93.

21. Victor Herbert, "Folic Acid and Vitamin B12," in *Modern Nutrition in Health and Disease*, ed. Robert S. Goodhart and Maurice E. Shils, 5th ed. (Philadelphia: Lea and Febiger, 1973), pp. 221-44.

22. D. M. Hegsted, "Major Minerals, Calcium and Phosphorus," in *Modern Nutrition in Health and Disease*, ed. Robert S. Goodhart and Maurice E. Shils, 5th ed. (Philadelphia: Lea and Febiger, 1973), pp. 268-86.

Chapter 3

Food and People

To eat or not to eat flesh is a question as old as the human race. Many of the 40 to 50 nutrients needed by the human body can be obtained from either animal or plant sources. With the exception of vitamin B_{12}, all known nutrients or their precursors are available from some form of plant life. From plants they are transferred to the bodies of animals, and thence to other animals.

In a few cases the plant form is the precursor of an essential nutrient. Vitamin A, as such, is found only in animal products, but carotene, from which vitamin A is produced in both human and animal bodies, is common in many vegetables and fruits. Vitamin A can therefore be obtained directly from animal products—liver, whole milk, cream, eggs—or in the form of carotene, the provitamin, from plant life, especially from deep green leafy vegetables and deep yellow vegetables and fruits.

Carbohydrate is found almost exclusively in plant sources, except for that in milk sugar from the various milks. Vitamin C is much more liberally supplied from fruits and vegetables than from animal products. A few other nutrients are encountered in larger quantities in animal or in plant sources, but most are available to some degree, at least, from both.

Figure 1. *The types of food nutrients essential to health*

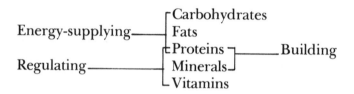

Energy Needs

Every activity of every cell in the body requires energy. It is essential to the cell's use of all of the other nutrients. Without energy from the energy-supplying foods, these other nutrients could not be absorbed, much less utilized.

Although proteins are included with the energy foods, the production of energy is not the only—nor even the primary—function of proteins. Their unique purpose is to provide building materials for bones and muscles, nerves, blood cells and antibodies, hormones and enzymes, skin, hair, and nails—indeed all tissues of the body. When these needs have been supplied, the non-nitrogenous remainder of the proteins is used—or stored—like the other energy substances. They may even be stored as body fat, along with the fat produced by excess carbohydrates and food fats.

If, however, the meals contain insufficient carbohydrates

and fats and the body is lacking in energy sources, then the proteins eaten are broken down to provide essential energy. This requirement must be satisfied first, and so the unique protein function of tissue building may, in this case, be lost.

In strictly energy terms fat and carbohydrate are interchangeable. The energy value of fat, however, is two-and-one-quarter times that of carbohydrate. A limited amount

Table 3. *Common Food Sources Providing Calories (Energy)*

	Plants	Dairy, Eggs	Meat, Fish, Poultry
Proteins	Legumes, (soy and other dried beans, peas, lentils, garbanzos, etc.). Nuts (amounts vary). Textured vegetable protein and meat analogs. Cereals and vegetables in lesser amounts.	Milk, cheese, eggs	All meat, fish poultry. Gelatin
Fats	Vegetable oils, nuts, olives, avocados. Salad dressings, vegetable shortenings and margarines.	Whole milk, cream, butter, most cheeses, egg yolk	Meat, fish, poultry, lard and other animal fats
Carbohydrates	Vegetables and fruits in varying amounts; breads and cereals, legumes, nuts. Sugars, syrups, molasses, honey, jams and jellies.	Lactose (milk sugar)	

of fat is important as a carrier of fat-soluble vitamins—A, D, E, and K—and at least one other substance, linoleic acid, found in several common food fats, is essential.

Some fats are highly visible; others are tucked away in unexpected places such as corn, from which comes corn oil. Two fruits well known for their fat content are olives and avocados. Although indistinguishable, fat is also a liberal component of egg yolk and homogenized whole milk. Carbohydrate, mostly in the form of starches and sugars, is found in practically all foods except fats and oils, meats, and eggs.

Protein is a component of almost all foods except fats and pure carbohydrates. The amount differs widely from 20 percent in lean meats to .5 percent in some fruits. It is low in vegetables, somewhat higher in cereals, and much higher in dried mature legumes. It is variable in nuts in both quantity and quality.

Minerals

Along with protein, various minerals help to build the body. They also help to keep the system functioning smoothly. One mineral may perform several vital functions. Calcium, phosphorus, and magnesium are necessary components of the bony structure, but they have many other equally vital uses. Calcium is essential to normal heart rhythm, nerve and muscle function, blood clotting, and the binding together of cells into tissues. Phosphorus is involved in almost every step of energy production and use, and is a key nutrient in maintaining the acid-alkaline balance of the body. It plays an important part in cell reproduction and the transmission of hereditary characteristics. Magnesium is vital to energy production and utilization, and to protein synthesis. It is involved in nerve and muscle activity and, like calcium but in a different way, is necessary to normal heart function. It also plays a part in regulation of body temperature.

Table 4. *Common Food Sources Providing Minerals*

	Plants	Dairy, Eggs	Meat, Fish, Poultry	Other
Calcium	Greens: mustard, turnip, dandelion, collards, kale, broccoli; almonds, sesame seeds; many fruits, vegetables, nuts, legumes in small amounts	Milk, cheeses, egg yolks	Sardines, salmon with bones as in canned salmon, small fish with bones included, oysters, shrimp, clams	
Phosphorus	Legumes, nuts, whole grains	Milk, cheese, eggs	Meat, fish, poultry	
Magnesium	Nuts, soybeans, whole grains, green leafy vegetables, legumes	Milk	Seafood, meat	
Sulfur	Legumes, nuts	Milk, cheese, eggs	Meat, fish, poultry	
Sodium	Small amounts in vegetables, especially green leafy, beets, carrots, celery, turnips	Milk, cheese, eggs	Meat, poultry, seafoods	Table and cooking salt (sodium chloride); all foods prepared or preserved with salt; soda, baking powder; food additives containing sodium
Potassium	Bananas, avocados, other fresh and dried fruits, vegetables, legumes, whole grains, nuts	Milk	Meat, fish, poultry	
Chloride*	Bananas, greens, celery, sweet potatoes, beets	Milk, eggs	Oysters, liver, heart, kidney, beef, lamb, poultry, seafoods	Table and cooking salt, all foods prepared with salt

*From: Henry C. Sherman, *Chemistry of Food and Nutrition,* 8th ed. (New York: Macmillan, 1952) pp. 682-87.

Other minerals required in relatively large amounts, and each performing more than one function, are sulfur (a component of several amino acids, B-vitamins, and hormones), sodium, potassium, and chlorine (chloride). These last three are vitally important to maintaining water balance within and outside the walls of billions of individual cells making up the body. They contribute to the normal acid base balance of the blood, which is essential to the well-being of the body. They play an important role in muscle function. Chloride, in the form of hydrochloric acid in the stomach, assists in the digestive breakdown of protein.

Other minerals are required in lesser amounts. These are the microminerals, sometimes called trace minerals. Their importance is entirely out of proportion to their minute requirements. They include iron, essential to good red blood and the avoidance of anemia. Iron is one of the nutrients most likely to be deficient in the diet, whether vegetarian or nonvegetarian.

Another micromineral is iodine, needed by the thyroid gland. Without it physical and mental development is regarded. Slight deficiencies may produce simple goiter and general physical and mental sluggishness. Extreme prenatal deficiencies, rarely seen today in some countries, produce severe malformation of infants.

Copper is essential to the utilization of iron, besides having an impressive list of functions in its own right. Copper deficiency from an inadequate dietary supply occurs, but it is one of the less common deficiencies, at least in a severe form. Perhaps its relative rarity is due to the variety of foods containing copper.

Other trace elements include cobalt, a component of vitamin B_{12}; zinc, with a variety of functions; fluorine, essential to sound tooth structure and perhaps to bones as well; manganese, chromium, molybdenum, and others about which much more information is needed.

Table 5. *Common Food Sources of Microminerals*

	Plants	Dairy, Eggs	Meat, Fish, Poultry	Other
Iron	Legumes, nuts, greens, limas, peas, tomato juice, dates, dried fruits, whole and enriched breads and cereals	Egg yolk	Meat (especially organ meats), poultry, seafoods	
Iodine	Vegetables grown on soil which is not iodine-deficient	Dependent upon animal rations	Seafoods; meat and poultry dependent upon animal rations	Iodized table salt
Copper	Legumes, nuts raisins, whole-grain cereals		Liver, kidney, shellfish	
Zinc*	Whole grains, legumes, peanuts	Milk, egg yolk	Meat, especially liver; seafoods, especially oysters; dark meat of chicken	
Fluorine	Minute amounts depending upon soil and environment		Seafoods consumed with the bones; minute amounts in meals, depending upon soil and feed	Water with natural or added fluorine content
Manganese	Whole grains, nuts, legumes	Although manganese is widely distributed, dairy products are relatively poor	Relatively poor	

---

*From: Jeanne H. Freeland and Robert J. Cousins, "Zinc Content of Selected Foods," *Journal of the American Dietetic Association* 68 (June 1976): 526-29; Kathryn A. Haeflein and Arlette I. Rasmussen, "Zinc Content of Selected Foods," *Journal of the American Dietetic Association* 70 (June 1977): 610-16; and E. W. Murphy, B. W. Willis, and B. K. Watt, "Provisional Tables on the Zinc Content of Foods," *Journal of the American Dietetic Association* 66 (April 1975):345-55.

There are traces of minerals in our food and in our bodies, the functions and values of which are still unknown, at least in terms of human nutrition. Some are recognized as essential in minute amounts, toxic in amounts only slightly larger.

Taken as a whole, minerals are essential to:
1. both soft and bony structures of the body
2. digestion and absorption of food
3. utilization of the energy available from energy foods
4. fluid and nutrient balance within and around the billions of individual cells of the body
5. good blood, with all its functions of oxygen delivery, ridding of waste products, etc.
6. normal acid and alkaline environment in the blood and digestive organs
7. nerve and muscle functioning
8. normal physical and mental development

Many of these functions are performed in cooperation with vitamins. No nutrient acts independently of others. Many processes are the result of two or three or more nutrients performing a vital task together. One example is the partnership between the mineral phosphorus and several B-vitamins, without which the body cells would soon be bereft of energy.

Vitamins

Vitamins were the last major class of nutrients to become known. In the early days of vitamin research these minute substances captured the public fancy as minerals had never done. They were not only powerful, but mysterious, often misunderstood or not understood at all. At times they were dramatic in their curative effects on deficiency diseases.

Like minerals, they have many functions. Vitamin A is necessary for normal growth of the skeleton, for healthy skin, cells, and body passages, for tooth development, and for normal vision. So important is vitamin A to the eye that an extreme deficiency, common in some parts of the world, results in blindness.

Table 6. *Common Food Sources of Vitamin A*

	Plants	*Dairy, Eggs*	*Meat, Fish, Poultry*
Vitamin A	(Carotene) Dark green leafy vegetables, deep yellow vegetables and fruits, fortified vegetable margarines	Whole milk, cream, butter, egg yolks, fortified nonfat milks	Liver

The B-complex vitamins include thiamin (B_1), riboflavin (B_2), niacin, pyridoxine (B_6), folacin, biotin, pantothenic acid, and cobalamin (B_{12}). The popular terminology for the B vitamins reflects their history. Thiamin, first to be discovered, is still often referred to as vitamin B_1, and riboflavin as vitamin B_2. Vitamin B_6 is found in three forms of approximately equal value, of which pyridoxine is merely one. Two forms are found largely in animal products, the third predominantly in plant life[1]. Vitamin B_{12} is among the most recently discovered nutrients.

Many, but not all, B-vitamin functions have to do with the production and use of energy from the energy-bearing foods. Folacin is essential to red blood cell formation, and vitamin B_{12} plays an important part in maintaining the central nervous system.

Table 7. *Sources of B-vitamins.*

	Plants	*Dairy, Eggs*	*Meat, Fish, Poultry*	*Other*
Vitamin B₁	Whole-grain and enriched bread, cereal, and flour products; legumes		Muscle meats, especially pork	
Riboflavin	Green leafy vegetables, whole-grain and enriched bread, flour and cereal products, legumes, nuts	Milk, cheese, eggs	Liver, heart, kidney, muscle meats	
Niacin	Whole-grain and enriched bread, cereal, and flour products (except corn); peanuts, peanut butter, legumes		Liver, meat, fish, poultry	(Tryptophan, an amino acid, can be converted into niacin in the body)
Vitamin B₆*	Whole-grain breads, cereals, and flours, bananas, avocados, peanuts, English walnuts, cabbage, cauliflower, peas, potatoes, sweet potatoes	Egg yolk	Liver, kidney, muscle meats, fish, chickens	

	Plants	Dairy, Eggs	Meat, Fish, Poultry	Other
Pantothenic acid	Nuts, whole grains, avocados, fresh vegetables	Egg yolk	Liver, kidney, heart, lean meats	Small amounts in most foods, but much may be lost in processing
Folacin	Green leafy vegetables, legumes, nuts, whole-grain cereals	Eggs	Liver, kidney, lean beef, veal	
Biotin	Legumes, nuts, cauliflower. Smaller amounts in other vegetables and some fruits	Egg yolks	Liver, kidney and other organ meats	Some synthesis by bacteria in intestinal tract
Vitamin B_{12}	Fortified meat analogs, fortified soy milks	Milk, cheese, eggs	Liver, meat, fish, poultry	

*From: Home Economics Research Report No. 36, August 1969, USDA, quoted in Robert S. Goodhart and Maurice E. Shils, eds., *Modern Nutrition in Health and Disease,* 5th ed. (Philadelphia: Lea and Febiger, 1973), pp. 212, 213.

Vitamin C is essential for the normal functioning of all cells. It provides a substance which helps hold the cells of blood vessel walls, the soft tissues, and the bony framework intact. It aids in the absorption and use of iron, and seems to play an active role with several other vitamins.

Vitamin C is found in citrus fruits, strawberries, papayas, cantaloupes, tomatoes, green peppers, and fresh raw green vegetables.

Vitamin D, the "sunshine vitamin," is formed by the action of sunlight on the skin. In some countries young children are provided with an additional supply through concentrates and fortified foods, especially milk. The vitamin may be found in small amounts in whole milk and eggs.

Vitamin E is an antioxidant; that is, it helps to protect the red blood cells, unsaturated fatty acids, and vitamin A from oxidizing agents. Much more, however, needs to be known about it. Some of the claims made for it in animal research have not been validated in human nutrition. Vitamin K is essential to blood clotting.

Table 8. *Source of Fat-Soluble Vitamins D, E and K*

	Plants	Dairy, Eggs	Meat, Fish, Poultry	Other
Vitamin D		Fortified milk products, small amounts in butter and egg yolk.	Fish liver oils, small amounts in animal liver, salmon, sardines	Action of sunlight on skin
Vitamin E	Vegetable oils, green leafy vegetables, wheat germ	Milk, egg yolk	Liver	
Vitamin K	Green leafy vegetables			Synthesis by micro organisms in intestinal tract

Excessive dosage with fat-soluble vitamins—A, D, E, and K—should be avoided. The reason is that the body tends to store fat-soluble vitamins, while excreting excess water-soluble nutrients. Heavy overdosages with vitamins A and D have been highly toxic. There is generally no danger from the use of foods naturally high in these nutrients. However, caution should probably be exercised in the heavy use of strongly fortified food combinations over an extended period of time.

No claim to completeness is made for the brief source lists in these pages. In general, commonly recognized top sources in each category are included. A blank space does not necessarily mean that the nutrient is totally lacking; it may indicate an unimportant source.

Meat, fish, and poultry are included for the purpose of comparison. Not included are condiments, except salt, and beverages other than milk and fruit or vegetable juices.

Except where otherwise credited, information in the preceding tables is based on, or adapted from, the following sources:

Bogert, L. Jean, George M. Briggs, and Doris Howes Calloway, *Nutrition and Physical Fitness*. 9th ed. Philadelphia: W. B. Saunders, 1973.

Church, Charles Frederick and Helen Nichols Church. *Food Values of Portions Commonly Used*. 12th ed. Philadelphia: J. B. Lippincott, 1975.

Composition of Foods: Raw, Processed, Prepared. Agriculture Handbook No. 8, Consumer and Food Economics Research Division, Agricultural Research Service, U. S. Dept. of Agriculture. Washington, D.C.: Revised December 1963.

Fleck, Henrietta. *Introduction to Nutrition*. 2d ed. New York: Macmillan, 1971.

Goodhart, Robert S. and Maurice E. Shils, eds. *Modern Nutrition in Health and Disease*, 5th ed. Philadelphia: Lea and Febiger, 1973.

Krause, Marie V. and Martha A. Hunscher. *Food, Nutrition and Diet Therapy*. 5th ed. Philadelphia: W. B. Saunders, 1972.

Lagua, Rosalinda T., Virginia S. Claudio, and Victoria F. Thiele. *Nutrition and Diet Therapy Reference Dictionary*. 2d ed. St. Louis: C. V. Mosby, 1974.

Nutritive Value of American Foods in Common Units. Agriculture Handbook No. 456, Agricultural Research Service, U.S. Dept. of Agriculture. Washington, D.C.: November 1975.

Robinson, Corinne H. and Marilyn R. Lawler. *Normal and Therapeutic Nutrition*, 15th ed. New York: Macmillan, 1977.

Schneider, Howard A., Carl E. Anderson, and David B. Coursin. *Nutritional Support of Medical Practice*, Hagerstown, Maryland: Harper and Ross, 1977.

Stare, Frederick J. and Margaret McWilliams. *Living Nutrition*, 2d ed. New York: Wiley, 1977.

Sources of Nutrients

Some essential nutrients are widespread in natural foods, but high in few or none. A number of trace elements are required in such small amounts that human requirements are still unknown. Some substances are toxic when consumed in excess. Therefore, a variety of common foods— fruits, vegetables, legumes, nuts, whole grains, with dairy products and eggs—following a pattern such as the Daily Four adapted to the vegetarian program (see chap. 4), is the best insurance the lacto-ovo-vegetarian can have against deficiencies and excesses. And there are adaptations for the total vegetarian.

Sources of some nutrients, especially those popular in the public eye, are generally well known by everyone with a fair knowledge of nutrition. Sources of others, especially those more recently recognized as important, are often the subject of mild disagreement. One person will list what he considers the best sources of a nutrient; another with equal standing will present a slightly different list. Several facts contribute to this variance. One test often applied to the importance of a source is its popularity in the meal patterns of Americans. Unit for unit, one source may provide less of a given substance than another less popular one. Yet it may be treated as a good source because the amounts consumed daily by many persons make it, for them, an adequate source.

Many trace minerals are dependent upon amounts in the soil or animal rations which sustain the living plants or animals. Plant variety, growing conditions, or the amount of sunlight absorbed may affect the nutrient content. Emphasis elsewhere in this chapter points up the lack of complete nutrition information available today.

Availability of Nutrients

Once the amount of a given nutrient is determined, there may still be a question about the ready availability of that nutrient to the human body. (Herein lies one of the reasons sometimes given for the use of animal products. The vegetarian, however, is as well able to obtain all needed nutrients as the nonvegetarian.)

For example, it is well known that most dark green leafy vegetables contain considerable calcium. What has not been completely determined is how much the oxalic acid in many of these same greens affects the absorption of calcium, which combines with the oxalic acid to form calcium oxalate. This compound apparently cannot be absorbed by the human gastrointestinal tract. It is known, however, that the amount of oxalic acid varies among the different greens and other foods. Only when it is comparatively high, as in spinach, chard, and several less well-known varieties, is it thought to effectively forestall absorption of the calcium.

Phytic acid, a phosphorus compound in nuts, legumes, and the bran layer of whole grains, may interfere with the utilization of calcium, magnesium, and iron. (Catherine F. Adams, *Nutritive Value of American Foods in Common Units*, Agriculture Handbook No. 456, Agricultural Research Service, U. S. Dept. of Agriculture, Washington, D.C.: 1975)

Zinc is another trace mineral which becomes unavailable in the presence of excess phytates. In yeast-raised whole grain breads, however, the enzyme phytase contained in the yeast alters the effect of the phytates, thus releasing some of the zinc.

Complexities in Nutrition

Remember, there are still many questions facing the nutritionist. We think, but are not quite sure, that we have discovered all the vitamins. We are more aware of the possibility that typical American diets may be low in some of the more recently discovered vitamins and in some minerals. In 1943 white bread and flour "enrichment" included thiamin, riboflavin, and niacin, along with iron. These were the major deficits in refined flours as recognized by the concerned and capable scientists studying the American food habits of that day. Today much more is known about other minerals and B-complex vitamins. Increased knowledge has not changed the picture; it has added to it. Practice, however, has not caught up; "enrichment" still consists of adding thiamin, riboflavin, niacin, and iron to white flour and bread. It would be most difficult to put back all nutrients which may be in short supply in highly refined diets. Even fiber, a nonnutritive substance, is now recognized as important. As a result, it makes sense to use whole-grain products in most cases.

Certain drugs have an effect on vitamin absorption and retention. The vitamin B_6 requirement, for example, seems to be increased by certain oral contraceptives.[2] Then there is the question of the importance of some trace minerals. Are they in the body because they are requirements and essential components of our food supply, or are they mere environmental contaminants? How many nutrients are toxic in excess amounts? How much is an excess?

Finally, there is the endless maze of nutrient interrelationships. Without adequate carbohydrate, or carbohydrate and fat, we cannot use protein as efficiently for its unique function of building tissues. Without an extensive assortment of vitamins and minerals we cannot use proteins, carbohydrates, nor fats. Calcium and phosphorus are useless for bonemaking without vitamin D. Copper, vitamin

B$_{12}$, and vitamin C are related to iron in the performance of its functions. The opposing effects of certain minerals, such as calcium on one side and the magnesium/sodium/ potassium combination on the other, are vital to normal nerve and muscle function, including the heart muscle. Other substances, particularly protein and phosphorus, are able to step in as buffers to maintain the normal acid-alkaline reactions of the blood and the other fluids.* Sometimes an excess of one nutrient seems to interfere with the presence and the functioning of another.

In the meantime we cannot sort and measure and mix nutrients to be certain we have just enough of each one and not too much of any. Occasionally we meet people who would like to do this. But each person is a unique individual with a unique physical makeup. He differs from every other individual around him. Some of this uniqueness is due to genetic factors, some to environment, some to lifestyle. One person is more active, or less active, physically or mentally, than another. One spends more time indoors, or outdoors, in the sun, or in the water.

Usually the closest we can come to exact nutritional requirements is through the use of tables based on average people with average needs. The well-known RDAs, the official United States recommended dietary allowances, are tables of nutrients recommended for specific age and sex groups. It is important to note that they are neither maximum nor minimum requirements. They do not include special (therapeutic) needs based on disease or other conditions, which occasionally may require more or less of given nutrients. Nutrients of which little is known as to probable requirements are not included.

---

*There is no relationship between the flavor of a food and its acid or alkaline ash, The volatile acids which provide the delightful tartness of oranges, grapefruit, strawberries, tomatoes, etc., do not contribute to the final product of acidity. Both acidity and alkalinity are produced by the ash of the corresponding minerals, all of which are essential nutrients. As long as the body remains in health the buffer system enables it to maintain a proper balance.

The RDAs were developed by the Food and Nutrition Board of the National Research Council and are revised every five years according to current scientific evidence. Sometimes nutrients are added to the list as more information about them becomes available. The 1973 RDAs were the first to include a recommended level of zinc. Sometimes recommendations are lowered, as in the 1973 allowances for protein and vitamin C.[3]

Although the RDAs are not to be interpreted as requirements, they can serve as guidelines when accompanied by, or used with, food tables showing nutrient content of various foods.

Nutritious Meals

The 1973 edition of Recommended Dietary Allowances emphasizes the need for a variety of foods to meet the RDA levels.[4] Very restricted dietaries may rule out more than one nutrient. "Freak" diets, some reducing diets, and consumption of heavily processed foods may shortchange the eater in important nutrients.

In fact, there are three requirements basic to a balanced, adequate meal pattern.

First it should be high in natural foods—whole-grain breads and cereals, and fruits and vegetables either fresh or processed without heavy amounts of sugar. Fruit juices, fresh, canned, or frozen, should be chosen far more than fruit-flavored beverages, no matter how high the vitamin C fortification of the beverages. Many commercially prepared foods, ranging from breakfast foods to entrees, contain an interesting alphabet of additives, but most of the initial goodness of the food has been processed away.

Second, and this factor has already been emphasized, is the use of a wide variety of foods. Just as for the adult no one food is indispensable, so no one food can provide all nutrients in optimal amounts. Sensible enrichment and fortification of some foods have done much for our health. There is, however, absolutely no advantage to obtaining 100 percent of five or ten or twenty "requirements" from one highly advertised food product. We are reminded of the little boy who refused to eat his spinach for lunch because, he asserted stoutly, he had consumed his day's requirements in his breakfast cereal. Use such foods occasionally if you wish, but by all means eat a wide range of foods which do not require fortification because they have not been highly refined in the first place.

Third is the elimination of "empty calories," foods consisting largely of pure carbohydrate, bulk, or fat, unaccompanied by minerals, vitamins, or protein. Few foods in their natural form consist of one nutrient only, although one often predominates. Whole wheat contains protein, fat, cellulose, phosphorus, and other minerals, vitamin E, and many members of the B-complex vitamins. Yet it is basically a carbohydrate food.

Sugar, on the other hand, is a concentrated carbohydrate, yielding little except energy. It should be used only as a flavoring and not as a staple.

The ideal vegetarian has a high regard for nutrition standards, and he also has a keen appreciation of the charming packages in which his favorite foods are brought to him. Hidden away in whole grains are many of the B-vitamins, vitamin E, iron, and other minerals. Iron is one of the strongholds of the nonvegetarian. But iron comes also in egg yolk, dried legumes, green leafy vegetables, and some dried fruits, including prunes, raisins, and apricots. Calcium is best known in milk, but it also comes to us along with the crisp texture of deep green leafy vegetables,* the crunchiness of nuts, in most members of the legume group, and even from a variety of our favorite fruits and vegetables.

---

*Exceptions include spinach, swiss chard, and lamb's-quarters, in which calcium is chemically combined with oxalic acid. In this form it apparently cannot be absorbed by the human digestive tract.

It is in fruits and vegetables that nature wields her most effective touch of beauty. Our grandmother's often unskilled handling of vegetables, overcooking them at every turn, left many people with a permanent dislike of these versatile bearers of vitamins and minerals. Modern methods and equipment are restoring their popularity.

Carotene, from which much of our vitamin A is formed, is found in the lively yellow and orange of carrots, yams, winter squash, apricots, peaches, and cantaloupes. It masquerades behind the deep green spinach, swiss chard, mustard greens, and others. Vitamin C is hidden within the many hues of red and green bell peppers, cantaloupes, strawberries, oranges, grapefruits, and lemons. The graceful golden banana is an excellent source of vitamin B_6 and a minor storehouse of other valuable nutrients.

In summary, a vegetarian diet, like its nonvegetarian counterpart, must yield 40 to 50 essential nutrients. These nutrients are provided abundantly through the many forms of plant life, supplemented with egg and dairy products, or, for the total vegetarian, with a limited number of fortified foods or vitamin supplements.

Food is, moreover, something to be enjoyed. Its colors, textures and flavors should help to make a dull day brighter, a bright day closer to perfection.

References

1. Howerde E. Sauberlich and John E. Canham, "Vitamin B_6," in *Modern Nutrition in Health and Disease*, ed. Robert S. Goodhart and Maurice E. Shils, 5th ed. (Philadelphia: Lea and Febiger, 1973), pp. 210-20.

2. Ibid.

3. Food and Nutrition Board, National Research Council, *Recommended Dietary Allowances*, 8th rev. ed. (Washington: National Academy of Sciences, 1974).

4. Ibid.

Chapter 4

Now for the Menu

Obviously, we cannot plan meals in terms of so much energy food, protein, and the dozens of vitamins and minerals important to us. What we can do is use the concept of food groups. Even though food groups alone are insufficient as a device to provide top-quality nutrition, accompanied by variety within groups they can be a tremendous help to planning.

For many years nutritionists have worked at developing food grouping devices to assist meal planners. As early as 1912 a five-group plan, including water as one of the groups, was published.[1] During World War I another five-group guide was recommended by government nutritionists to help homemakers cope with problems of food

61

rationing. Carbohydrates were divided into two groups, starches and sugars.[2]

During World War II the Basic Seven was popular. Later on the Basic Seven was simplified, and Food for Fitness, a four-group guide, came into everyday use.[3] Both the Basic Seven and the Food for Fitness patterns have been adapted to lacto-ovo-vegetarian use. Since no food grouping system by itself can assure nutritional adequacy, these devices are widely published and used for a time, then discarded in favor of another, and supposedly more effective, pattern.

Most of the vegetarian adaptations of the Food for Fitness (Daily Four) guides include all four groups: dairy products, protein foods, breads and cereals, and fruits and vegetables with their two subgroups—citrus fruits and dark green leafy vegetables. Meat is omitted from the protein group; legumes and nuts are retained, and meat analogs are usually added. Soy beverages and soy cheese may be added to the dairy group; this gives the total vegetarian a nondairy choice. The numbers of daily servings are generally the same: one pint or more of dairy milk, or equivalents in cheese or other dairy products, for adults, and larger amounts of milk for children and teenagers; at least two protein servings; four or more slices of whole-grain or enriched bread, or the equivalent in cereals; and four or more servings of fruit and vegetables, including the citrus and dark green leafy groups.

The Daily Four is generally considered a safe guide for lacto-ovo-vegetarians. It would be helpful, however, to have a slightly more detailed guideline, although any additions will make it that much more complicated. Much of its present value is due to its simplicity. For the lacto-ovo group it may be sufficient to emphasize the wide range of plant foods. Frequent use of high-iron dried fruits—apricots, peaches, prunes, dates, raisins, and currants—is important. Another important group includes deep yellow vegetables and fruits, such as fresh, canned and frozen carrots, winter squash, sweet potatoes, peaches, and apricots.

The total vegetarian will need a dependable source of vitamin B_{12} and perhaps of vitamin D. Fortified soy beverages provide vitamin B_{12} and often other nutrients also. Persons accustomed to dairy milk will not immediately enjoy "soy milk" in its plain form. It can, however, be used in cooking and in delicious imitation milk or fruit shakes such as banana, date, or strawberry. Most meat analogs also provide vitamin B_{12} through fortification.

Although enrichment of breads, flours, and cereals has undoubtedly done much for the health of many persons, more emphasis should be placed on the use of whole-grain products. They need not be used to the exclusion of all enriched, refined products, but they should be much more generally used than they are now.

These additional suggestions would surely be good for all to follow, both vegetarians and nonvegetarians.

For the present it might be advisable to place meat analogs in a separate group. They are not essential in a vegetarian diet and they are not always convenient to obtain, but they do provide variety and are often well liked.

These foods are made from various substances including wheat, soy beans, peanuts, etc. Some are processed to imitate meats, poultry, or fish as, for example, wiener-like products. They contain less cholesterol (generally none at all) and saturated fatty acids than do meat and meat products. Buyers should read the can or package labels to determine the extent of fortification and whether they contain combinations of ingredients to increase their protein values. It is not necessary that they be fortified to the exact level of meat products. When they are better known and more widely available they will be a convenient addition to the other vegetable proteins.

Two other food groups, not included in the Daily Four,

are sugars and concentrated fats. They should be used sparingly. Too large intakes of either can quickly dull appetites, crowd out more nourishing protective foods, and in some cases even contribute to disease conditions.

Any diet too low in fat or protein may result in lack of a sense of satiety, with a resulting urge for more food intake. If this desire is indulged there will probably be a gain in weight. Nuts, which are high in fat, will help to provide the sense of satiety. In this case nuts should be a planned part of the meal and not a high-calorie afterthought.

Attitudes Toward Food and Their Effects on Planning

It has been said that Americans often make a moral issue out of food. This food is *good*; that food is *bad*. Children undoubtedly experience this method in full force. This (disliked) food is "good for you," that (delicious) substance "is bad for you." For the time being the child may be required to comply; the day comes all too soon when he is no longer a child but a teenager or a young adult, free, mobile, and sufficiently affluent to do as he chooses. Basic food preferences, likes and dislikes, are learned early in life, often as a result of pleasant and unpleasant experiences. A knowledge of nutrition is acquired later if it is ever acquired at all. One purpose of food group guidelines is to help develop good food habits with a minimum of effort.

There are two extremes to avoid, and it would be difficult to determine which is the more destructive to healthful eating patterns. Both dangers are illustrated by two persons consulting a dietitian for help with their problems. The first was a middle-aged woman who said that she had been unable to persuade her husband to eat as she thought he should, and she was enlisting the aid of the dietitian to help educate him. Both husband and wife were lacto-ovo-vegetarians. The lady's first question was "How much cottage cheese should a person eat?"

"As much as you like," responded the dietitian. "It is a good protein food, but there is no specific recommended amount. It's just a matter of how much you want to eat. One should not try to live on cottage cheese alone for protein."

But the questioner was not at all satisfied. "I need to know," she insisted, "how many tablespoons of cottage cheese a day we should eat."

She had another problem. "My husband objects to baked potatoes. Of course, the only way to get all the nutrition in a potato is to bake it. How can I get him to accept baked potatoes?"

She complained of having to carry on a continuous battle to provide healthful meals which her husband emphatically resisted. The reason was obvious. Food in that home was not a delight, but a stern and rigid duty.

The other person was a woman who wished to become a total vegetarian. As the dietitian pointed out the various food groups all went well until the bread-cereal group was mentioned.

"I can't eat any breads or cereals," said the woman. "The doctor says they are bad for my arthritis."* And right there the matter stalled. A reduction in intake of this group would certainly not have exceeded the dietitian's skill. But to completely eliminate the whole group with its vitally important store of minerals and vitamins seemed impossible on the heels of eliminating the entire lacto-ovo group.

Planning With Food Groups

Providing a variety of foods from meal to meal and from day to day does not mean continuously searching for ex-

---

*Half a century ago a low carbohydrate diet was used experimentally for the treatment of some cases of arthritis. It was later judged ineffective and its use discontinued. It has since been used occasionally by individual physicians.

pensive, exotic, or out-of-season foods. It does mean varying protein foods, using more than one kind and color of vegetable, obtaining as much fruit (especially fresh) as possible, using dried fruits (which are often ignored), and varying preparation methods to include some raw fruits and vegetables.

The meat-eating adult will easily consume between 14 and 30 grams of protein in meat, poultry, or fish at a meal. Depending upon his consumption of other foods throughout the day, the total amount may be less than, equal to, or in excess of the recommended daily allowance. For the heavy meat eater it will be considerably in excess.

Meals are nutritional units. The more protein eaten as meat, milk, legumes, nuts, or manufactured foods, the less dependence will be placed on the protein of cereals and vegetables. But cereals and vegetables are themselves essentials, and should not be ignored. And the total vegetarian will need their supplementary protein value to complete his essential amino acid intake.

For the beginning vegetarian the meat analogs, when available, are often a help. They come in such a range of styles and flavors that each person must determine his own favorites. Many can be used in meat recipes such as a la king dishes, meat loaf-like entrees, noodle and spaghetti dishes, and sandwiches. Recipes are generally available from the manufacturers.

It may seem wonderfully strange to the meat lover, but many a confirmed vegetarian will smack his lips as loudly over a cup of lentils as will his neighbor over a luscious slice of roast chicken. Protein content of either is slightly over 11 grams.[4]

If the lentils are imaginatively cooked and seasoned by a practiced vegetarian cook, the meat eater will also smack his lips over the lentils, though he will still eat the chicken (thereby increasing his protein intake to 23 grams). There are over a dozen legumes on the market: beans of several varieties, soy beans, garbanzos, split peas, lentils, and peanuts (popularly included with nuts, but actually a legume).

Many vegetarian entrees are made in loaf or pattie form with nuts, cereal, eggs, and seasonings. Quality and quantity of protein varies; nuts, like other plant proteins, are best combined with other foods to obtain the higher biological values of which vegetable proteins are capable. Naturally an entree containing eggs and/or milk or milk powder will contain the equivalent of a high-quality protein even though the nut base is low. Moreover, many vegetarians are as fond of nuts as the nonvegetarian is of meat. They eat them accordingly, consuming an appreciable amount of protein and worry as little over cost or calories.

Four or five fruits and vegetables are a daily minimum. Indeed, it is difficult if not impossible to obtain sufficient vitamins and minerals, including trace minerals, without an abundance of fruits and vegetables. In this area the vegetarian has a considerable advantage over many nonvegetarians, who often treat this class of foods as mere accompaniments, or, at best, as between-meal snacks.

Whole grains, breads and cereals are important to the vegetarian plan. Their contributions vary with the basic cereal, but as consumed in the United States they generally contribute several B-complex vitamins, vitamin E, phosphorus, iron, potassium, and essential amino acids (other than lysine and threonine, which are present in insufficient amounts).

Refined cereal products have lost much of their vitamin and mineral content, and some of their protein value. In the enriched varieties, four nutrients have been returned: thiamin, riboflavin, niacin, and iron. Many of the popular prepared cereals have received additional enrichment or fortification, sometimes extending to vitamins not naturally contained in cereals, such as vitamins B_{12} and D. The overall nutritional picture is the important factor and here the advantage generally lies with the whole-grain product. Cereal products, especially the whole-grain varieties, add considerably to the protein intake during a three-meal period.

It is important that sufficient food be included in the first meal of the day. Approximately one-third of the recommended protein allowance, with sufficient energy foods for predicted activity levels, should be eaten. Essential mineral and vitamin requirements will be met if the protein and energy foods are well chosen from such natural foods as whole-grain breads and cereals, legumes, nuts, fresh and processed fruits, milk, and perhaps eggs. Total vegetarians will replace eggs and milk with additional nuts, legumes, and perhaps meat analogs. They should also keep in mind possible cereal and/or flour combinations which increase the biological value of the protein.

Remember that the vegan diet will require some supplements, including vitamin B_{12}, and often vitamin D and iodine (nonvegetarians may also lack the latter two). Iodine needs can be met by the use of iodized salt. Remember also that children and pregnant or nursing mothers are always at greater risk than other healthy persons.

The amounts of vitamin D found in unfortified dairy products and eggs are usually too small to provide for growing bodies. Consequently, most fluid milks, butter, and margarines are fortified with this vitamin. The ultimate natural source, sunlight, is often rendered inadequate by climate, air pollution, and indoor lifestyles. Vitamin D supplementation is uniformly recommended for infants and very young children. Older children can easily obtain their requirements from fortified milk. Total vegetarians, however, do not use milk nor give it to their children. Here, obviously, some other source of vitamin D must be found.

Four hundred international units (I.U.) are the recommended daily standard for children, adolescents and nursing mothers. Recommendations for other adults beyond the early twenties have not been made, since it is assumed they will obtain their needs through sunlight on the skin. Nonanimal sources of vitamin D include: fortified meat analogs, fortified soy beverages, and vitamin D supplements.

The supplements may require a physician's prescription. Heavy overdosage with vitamin D over a prolonged time period is highly toxic. Fatalities are not unknown. But the vitamin can safely be taken in smaller doses. Except for circumstances determined by a qualified health practitioner, it should never be taken in amounts exceeding 400 international units (I.U.) as a daily allowance.

There is one substance which vegetarians have no problem consuming—fiber. There is increasing evidence that the healthy digestive tract needs more fiber than the popular American diet contributes. Added research will provide sound facts where we must often now evaluate statistical evidence. The vegetarian's consumption of fruits and vegetables, whole grains, nuts, and legumes greatly increases the fiber intake over that of the average nonvegetarian. Some evidence, largely statistical, is currently interpreted to indicate that a considerable increase in fiber may cut down on several common diseases and disease conditions ranging from appendicitis and hemorrhoids to coronary heart disease and colon cancer. One interesting discovery involved vitamin B_{12}. In certain cases where no known vitamin B_{12} had been ingested, an increase in fiber consumed appeared to result in increased stores of the vitamin.[5]

Today vegetarians and vegetarianism have undergone much study. Perhaps the first really intensive investigation in the United States was that of Hardinge and Stare, reported in 1954.[6] Two hundred subjects included three groups—nonvegetarian, lacto-ovo, and total vegetarian. Careful blood tests revealed no evidence of deficiency in any of the groups. All subjects met or exceeded the RDAs of the early 1950s. These early tables did not include the newly discovered vitamin B_{12}.

From all the evidence available today vegetarians have at the least an equal chance for abundant health with any group of people in today's world. The first step toward this lifestyle is to take advantage of nature's own plant food groups with their almost endless varieties of shapes, colors, textures, flavors, and nutritional characteristics.

The Finished Menu

So how to plan the menu?

First, the beginning meal of the day should be a substantial one. It need not be time-consuming in preparation, although cooking a hot cereal requires more time than pouring a cold one. Additional whole-grain bread or toast could be substituted for the hot cereal on busy days when the family must be up and away at an early hour. And the best and most natural of the prepared cereals can sometimes be used. Ideally for most persons the meal will include a whole-grain cereal, bread or toast, at least two fruits (one may be a juice), and a nourishing beverage. Milk, or fortified soy milk, if preferred, may be served cold, hot or in an unsweetened beverage. The overall meal should be low in sugar and at least moderately low in fats. A delectable fruit, fresh, canned, or dried, is preferable to jelly or jam. Skim milk contains only a little more than half the calories of whole milk. The vitamin value of whole milk is easily obtained elsewhere. The total vegetarian will prefer soy to dairy milk. Be sure to check the label for facts about fortification.

But there is absolutely no reason why a breakfast must be

based on cereal and toast. If your family prefers peanut butter and date sandwiches, or toast with beanut butter and apple sauce, and you can provide them, why not serve them? Make them of whole-grain bread and let your family enjoy them. Or perhaps they prefer a fruit plate with a not-too-sweet special bread and a hot milk or soy milk beverage.

The main meal of the day may be built around an entree—loaf, patties, casserole, legumes, meat analog—or it may consist of an attractive salad or sandwich, or the two in combination, accompanied by one or more vegetables or fruits. The third meal may follow the same general pattern or it may be completely different. It may be a lighter meal, both in quantity and content. Total amount of food and calories for the day should be considered in planning. Excess calories will soon show up in weight gain, a condition often difficult to reverse once it is started.

The day's total should include two or three protein foods other than milk or soy milk, at least five fruits and vegetables, some form of bread or cereal at most meals, and two or more glasses of milk (more for older children, teenagers, and pregnant women). It is important to include a variety of fruits and vegetables, with one citrus or high vitamin C fruit daily and deep green leafy and deep yellow vegetables several times a week. Thus, the main meal of the day might consist of lentil loaf with tomato sauce, brown rice, spinach, shredded raw carrot salad, and wheat germ cookies. The third meal, whether served at noon or evening, could include an egg and olive sandwich, potato salad with sliced tomatoes, melon, cashew nuts, and milk.

Attractive Vegetarian Meals

Obviously, not every meal can be "a thing of beauty." Not only are cost factors restrictive, but the family meal planner must handle many other time-consuming tasks and accomplish much more for loved ones than feeding them. Nevertheless, a word about attractive food at home is in order.

From the purely visible standpoint, two factors—color and shape—stand out. Variety is said to be the spice of life. Like any other spice, uninhibited variety can result in confusion instead of desirability. Colors should harmonize and not clash. If quarrelsome colors must be served at the same meal—one family member dotes on tomatoes and another on beets—serve them on separate dishes or at least with a neutral color element such as spinach between. Avoid garnishes which embarrass the rest of the plate or any part of it, such as parsley next to cooked green string beans. On the other hand, the green of peas, the yellow of carrots, and the white of fluffy whipped potatoes will combine effectively.

Sizes and shapes should vary. If baked potatoes are part of the meal, do not use an entree which too closely resembles the potato in size, shape, and color. Other vegetables could be sliced or cubed, and mashed.

Plates should not be too full or too empty. Especially when serving a limited amount of food, as in a weight control diet, arrange the foods together tastefully, with an edible, even though low-calorie, garnish.

A meal may be extremely simple, perhaps only a sandwich and soup or a beverage. It can still be neatly and attractively arranged with a simple garnish such as a carrot strip or curl, or a few fresh onion or green pepper rings. The sandwiches can be cut in different ways. The sandwich-salad plate is slightly more complicated, but extremely simple ingredients skillfully blended and arranged may be very attractive.

There is no question that vegetarian meals can be made just as attractive to the eye as those menus built around meat, fish, and poultry. Indeed, given the broad range of colors in fruits and vegetables, they can often be made more attractive. Non-meateaters have had the amusing experience of requesting—somewhat self-consciously, perhaps —vegetarian meals at a professional luncheon meeting, only to face the envious glances of their table mates who must do with the hotel's standard shrimp salad on tomato, with rolls, coffee, and dessert. Or perhaps it was hot turkey sandwich with gravy and french fries day. Whatever it was, it seemed entirely suitable until the arrival of those gaily hued fruit or vegetable plates.

Textures also should vary, so the entire meal does not consist entirely of soft, mushy foods or hard, crisp, and crunchy foods. Flavors should be combined like true soul mates, the pungent and the bland, the strong and the gentle, the heady and the weak.

With a bit of practice the meal planner begins to think in terms of color, shape, texture, arrangement, and flavor combinations. It becomes almost as much a habit to plan in these terms as to include the various and sometimes conflicting family likes and dislikes in the routine preparation of food. In fact, attention to the factors of color, shape, arrangement, texture, and flavor may help in overcoming some previous food dislikes. Finally, in the actual preparation and cooking of meals every effort should be made to conserve these qualities as well as the original nutritional values of the food.

In this chapter you have read about some suggested vegetarian menus. They may or not appeal to you, but they are far from being the only menus possible. Plan some others of your own. There are thousands of food combinations meeting the nutritional requirements.

During the week vary your fruits, vegetables, and protein foods. Use part of the milk (or soy milk), if you wish, in soups, casseroles, creamed vegetables, and simple desserts. Or substitute mild cheeses for part of the milk. Avoid foods low in everything but calories, i.e., high sugar and high fat dishes. Make the meals as attractive and colorful as possible.

References

1. Winifred Gibbs, *Economical Cooking, Planned for Two or More Persons* (New York: The New York Book Company, 1912).

2. Caroline L. Hunt and Helen W. Atwater, *How to Select Foods. I. What the Body Needs*, U.S. Department of Agriculture, Farmers' Bulletin No. 808 (Washington: Government Printing Office, 1917).

3. U. S. Department of Agriculture. Agricultural Research Service. Institute of Home Economics, *Food for Fitness, a Daily Food Guide*, Leaflet No. 424 revised (Washington: Government Printing Office, 1967).

4. Charles Frederick Church and Helen Nichols Church, *Food Values of Portions Commonly Used*, 12th ed. (Philadelphia: J. B. Lippincott, 1975), pp. 61, 81.

5. U. D. Register, "Fiber—the Edible Indigestible," Lecture, Nutrition Seminar. Nutrition and Dietetics Alumni Association, Loma Linda University, Loma Linda, California, March 24, 1977.

6. Mervyn G. Hardinge and Frederick J. Stare, "Nutritional Studies of Vegetarians, Pt. 1, Nutritional, Physical and Laboratory Studies," *The American Journal of Clinical Nutrition* 2 (March-April 1954): 73-82.

Chapter 5

The Littlest Vegan:
A Nonmeat Diet
For Infancy

Sooner or later someone is going to ask: How about the total vegetarian diet for pregnant mothers and young children? The lacto-ovo-vegetarian plan is so similar nutritionally to the nonvegetarian that it is recognized as safe for both mother and child. But is a diet excluding all animal products, and fortified with certain missing nutrients, including vitamin B_{12}, safe during the prenatal period when a new body is being formed, when bone and muscle, nerve and brain, and a host of other cells, are rapidly developing into a human being? Tests on animals indicate that early nutritional deprivation often impairs adult performance. This is an unthinkable risk to take with a human life.

75

Adequacy vs. Inadequacy

The total vegetarian diet can be adequate or it can be totally inadequate. There is, therefore, a grave risk, but it is one produced by human fallibility. We tend to be so sure of ourselves and yet so careless.

Throughout the centuries preceding the advance of nutrition knowledge, many infants and young children, and countless adults as well, went to early graves from scurvy, or beriberi, or pellagra, or some other disease now known to be the result of a nutritional deficiency. Today, in poorly fed areas of the world, much the same thing may happen. And in the United States of America, in the third quarter of the twentieth century, malnourished babies and toddlers of extremist, pseudovegetarian parents are sufficient evidence of the peril of a philosophical, or even a religious zeal, in the absence of an equal measure of wisdom. For the lack of carrying out a few simple rules of child-feeding—the inclusion of foods containing essential nutrients—some children have been doomed to malnutrition and its consequences.[1] One mother, in a few weeks or months or years, can prevent the normal physical and perhaps mental development of the child for whom she would undoubtedly sacrifice her life.

The adult on a total vegetarian diet must eat with care. It is not enough to believe in this way of life: the believer must obtain between 40 and 50 nutritional essentials. And that which is inadequate for the adult is totally insufficient for the small child. The body will not settle for less than its full share of nutrients. The earlier the age at which deprivation occurs, the more serious the consequences may be.

It is for this reason that so many nutritional specialists affirm their belief in the safety of the properly fortified total vegetarian diet and at the same time urge the inclusion of dairy products in the diets of small children.

Milk is one way, and an easy one, to meet certain nutritional needs. It is not the only way. There are babies, born with severe milk allergies, who thrive on a fortified soy milk-based diet. And scientists in some countries have put together combinations of plant products which have done much to combat malnutrition among children born in those countries. From such examples, and others, it is clear that animal products are not essential.

Much depends upon the wisdom and skill of the mother. The inability of infants to eat, digest, and utilize adult foods is obvious; when breastfeeding ends, satisfactory forms of adequate nourishment must be found and applied. Cultural food habits may be helps or hindrances, depending upon their particular nutritional significance.

Future research and the practical application of its findings will advance the progress already made. The experimental status of some recent nutrition research requires additional time to raise it to the level of everyday assured safe usage. For example, a blend of certain plant proteins has been found to equal milk protein as a growth agent.[2] But how is this blend to be produced, marketed, and used in the feeding of infants? It must be not only scientifically proven, but economically feasible and culturally acceptable.

There are also pitfalls in translating the results of animal feeding tests to humans. Although the similarities stand out, there are occasional differences as well. Research with human infants and young children is limited to studies of groups known to have lived under certain environmental conditions, including food and feeding patterns, and to situations where it is certain that any experimental variable will not do harm to a child.

Measures to Assure Safety

The mother today who aspires to bring up her child on a total vegetarian program must follow five vitally important steps, based on a solid rock of currently demonstrable fact:

1. Obtain nutritional information and guidance from qualified, known specialists in the field of nutrition, or from health practitioners with adequate nutrition training. These persons should be members of exacting scientific and/or professional organizations. These requirements will help to protect the mother from unwise or uninformed counsel.

2. The mother-to-be must maintain a well-rounded diet, including supplementation as advised by her physician, through pregnancy and breast feeding.

Ideally, a high level of nutrition will precede pregnancy. Then, especially during the latter half of the period, needs for most nutrients are increased. The mother who does not wish to use dairy milk during this time must obtain the protein, calcium, riboflavin, vitamin B_{12}, and all the other contributions of milk, from alternate sources. She may need additional supplements such as iron and vitamin D, as do most nonvegetarians. When she is nursing her baby, some of her needs will be increased to even higher levels.

3. Infants and toddlers must be fed according to directions provided by a qualified pediatrician acquainted with, though not necessily a follower of, the total vegetarian system. This feeding program will include an alternate product to replace dairy milk when the child is no longer breast-fed.

From the child's birth on, the pediatrician, or a responsible aide or assistant, will advise the mother on all aspects of the diet. It may not be advisable or even possible, to feed all infants the same foods or formulas. The times for addition of solid foods, and the best choices among these foods, are matters within the pediatrician's field. As more studies are conducted, more information becomes available, new products appear on the market, old products are altered in accordance with new standards, and the result is improved feeding practices. One current example is the decreased use of salt in strained vegetables for infant feeding.

4. As the child develops into a preschool and school-age youngster, his meals must include all essential food types—cereals, especially whole-grain, a variety of fruits including citrus, green leafy and other vegetables, proteins, and a fortified soy-milk product. The counsel of qualified specialists is still important. The occasional child with food allergies or food-related metabolic disorders must, of course, be under the long-term care of a competent physician.

5. Mealtimes must be happy times when the younger family members learn to enjoy a variety of healthful, tasty, attractive foods. Children should not be forced to eat things they particularly dislike. Many items will gradually become popular as the child grows in taste and perception. Young children often dislike mixtures, but love plain finger foods.

*   *   *

The next child, and the next, will hardly require so much effort on the part of the mother to learn the ABCs of their care and feeding. But each and every child has the same right to a safe, nourishing, and satisfying mealtime program during his growing years.

References

1. Darla Erhard, "The New Vegetarians, Pt. 1: Vegetarianism and its Medical Consequences," *Nutrition Today* 8 (November-December 1973): 4-12.

2. M. Narayana Rao and M. Swaminathan, "Plant Proteins in the Amelioration of Protein Deficiency States," in *World Review of Nutrition and Dietetics*, vol. 11, ed. Geoffrey H. Bourne (Basel, Switzerland and New York: S. Karger, 1969), pp. 106-41.

Chapter 6

Why the Vegetarian Life Style?

Many a nonvegetarian—parent, spouse, dietitian, restaurant manager, school food service director—has a responsibility for the care and feeding of vegetarians. This person probably never asked for the task of planning and preparing nourishing meatless meals and must sometimes wonder: What do these vegetarians see in their way of life? Why do they punish themselves, and me, with this eating pattern?

There are almost as many reason for vegetarianism as there are groups practicing it. Most motives, however, can be classified within three general types of interest patterns or basic beliefs: (1) economic and humanitarian, (2) health and environmental, and (3) religious and philosophical.

81

Humanitarian Motives

A primary reason for the recent upsurge of interest in meatless meals is the increasing awareness of hunger in many parts of the world. Unsolved economic, technological, and ultimately explosive population problems are perceived as time bombs about to go off. A short but severe drought, a flood, a greater than usual invasion of pests, a local war, and the limited resources become more limited until, without immediate outside help, thousands starve.

This is the shocking climax of which the wealthy world, through its roving news media, becomes immediately aware. But there is a continuous and perhaps greater tragedy day by day. This is the widespread deprivation of essential nutrients, the physical weakness, the infections and blindness and retardation which are the only birthright many receive.

"Let them starve," say some. "Feed them now and you are condemning future generations to greater suffering."

"Stop the population explosion," demand others and proceed to prove it can be done—in the advanced countries.

"Feed them," implores the third group. "There is sufficient land, and we have the technology."

The first solution is unthinkable, the second inadequate, the third almost impossible to carry out. A scientific and humanitarian combining of the second and third offers hope. It is a hope not easily realized, but it is worth our mightiest efforts.

It is true that many parts of the earth's surface are underutilized for food production. Large areas of these underdeveloped tracts would involve astronomical development costs, however.

Water is one of the prime limiting factors.[1] Neither plant nor animal life is possible without water. One writer has estimated the amount required to produce high-grade meat protein. Based on plant uptake of water, he sets a theoretical minimum of 300 gallons a day to provide food and comfort for a man consuming plant food only—a total vegetarian. Most of the water will be used, directly or indirectly, by the living plants. The man will then consume the plants. He will require some additional water for drinking and for cleanliness. But to provide high-quality steaks and roasts the food chain must be lengthened. Now the steer consumes much of the plant food, perhaps 25 to 35 pounds of alfalfa per day. With the inclusion of the steer's drinking water—a modest 12 gallons—the amount of water needed to provide this meat diet and the additional water for the man's other basic needs rises to 2500 gallons per day. The man now has a mixed diet consisting of plant and animal foods together, at a total environmental cost of approximately eight times the amount of water needed for his daily living as a total vegetarian.[2]

It is a fact that some plant foods, when consumed directly, provide much more protein per unit of land area than the steer. In some countries a large part of the grain and soybean production is used to feed animals. Someone has estimated that soybeans, admittedly not our most popular plant protein source, will supply at least 16 pounds of amino acids, milk about two pounds, and beef less than one pound per acre.[3] There is no question that meat production, except that carried on as a waste utilization process, i.e., the family pig and chickens, or the limited number of sparse range-fed animals, is extravagant in terms of resources.

Under the present system there is, naturally, a powerful problem of logistics. Who can effect the transfer of vital nutrients from a sophisticated consumer to a needy mouth in a faraway land? Who will guarantee delivery to a nutritionally deficient area of the world the caloric equivalent of the fat steer? How can the soil and water now nourishing the steer be put to better use than providing meat dishes?

Nevertheless, minds concerned with human hunger

around the globe see an end to heavy meat consumption, with its extravagant accompanying waste of increasingly scarce resources, as an important early step toward reaching a world-wide solution.[4]

Health Motives

A second widespread rationale is based on the natural desire for a superior level of health. Here we must beware that we are not being conned into some dusty form of age-old quackery or, equally objectionable, some new and shiny fad. Herein lie many of the reasons for questions about the safety of vegetarianism. Many are aware that young children have been permanently damaged physically and psychologically by extreme eating habits—but the damage was not brought about by vegetarianism.

In 1965, for example, the death of a young woman in a northeastern community alerted authorities to the dangers of extreme adherence to the Zen macrobiotic diet. For six months or more this young woman had eaten almost nothing but cereal, chiefly brown rice. Progressive weakness, weight loss, signs of scurvy and other evidence of extreme malnutrition all failed to dampen her enthusiasm for, or dim her faith in, the dietary regimen which, she believed, would soon restore her to complete health.[5]

In 1972, a *Newsweek* article reported there were 10,000 followers of this system in the United States. Fortunately few of them followed it to the death. According to the article, there were many malnourished children whose parents had adopted the Zen macrobiotic system and were receiving grossly inadequate intakes of protein, vitamin C, and other nutrients.[6] All of these nutrients could have been included in an entirely adequate form in either a lacto-ovo-vegetarian or a total vegetarian diet.

It is true that too many of our popular foods are refined and that preparation methods can make a vast difference in the nutritive qualities of a finished product. And there certainly are harmful additives still in use. But none of these problems requires that the individual take a drastic or extreme approach to his personal diet. Excellent foods are widely available in many forms.

Scientifically valid objections to meat eating include at least four factors: (1) animal diseases capable of being transmitted to humans, (2) excretory products remaining in the bloodstream after the animal's death, (3) chemical substances of unproved safety used in feed or as preservatives, and (4) the fat of red meats, high in cholesterol and saturated fatty acids.

Thorough cooking will do much to minimize the first factor, although we cannot be sure yet that reasonable heat treatment will destroy all disease-producing organisms, including viruses. Inspection, required by law, is a big help but does not provide complete safety. A few years ago many of us were startled and sickened to learn that cancerous animals were processed for food after removal of the visibly affected part. Trichinosis, common from the eating of pork, is somewhat less prevalent now than formerly. Pigs were once routinely fed on raw garbage and pork products were often consumed without adequate heat treatment. The result was widespread human infection. Equally commonplace was salmonella infection, an explosive but fortunately brief and seldom fatal illness. All animal products are subject to salmonella. Poultry and poultry products have been especially affected, in part, at least, by the practice of feeding animal byproducts to poultry. Here, as with trichinosis, some improvement has occurred through heat treatment of the feed. The dangers, however, have not been entirely removed. Other problems past or present include tularemia from rabbits, tapeworm from beef and fish, and brucellosis from meat and milk. This disease factor is probably one of the chief reasons behind many total vegetarians' refusal of all dairy and egg products. They believe that no animal product can be entirely disease free.

Thorough meat cooking, milk pasteurization, nonuse of raw eggs—all will help, admits the vegetarian, but why should he eat that which he does not want?

Excretory products remaining in the blood stream after death were doubtless lessened considerably by the prescribed Hebrew method of bleeding. While ridding the body of certain unwanted substances, this bleeding would hardly contribute to a high-quality market product according to the taste buds and texture feelers of most modern palates. More merciful slaughtering methods have lessened this problem, but cannot eliminate it entirely.

There is much discussion about the use of chemicals in rearing animals for slaughter and for the preservation of their flesh. Diethylstilbesterol, a chemical believed to have caused human cancer, has probably received the most attention. It is most difficult to eliminate products such as these because of their commercial benefits and the absence of effective substitutes. Laws attempting to curtail the use of these chemicals just before slaughter are not easily enforceable.

The public press has carried many warnings regarding the fat content of meats with its high accompaniment of cholesterol and saturated fatty acids. Both seem rather closely linked to atherosclerosis and coronary heart disease. Both cholesterol and saturated fatty acids are also rather high in butter, cream and whole milk. Egg yolks are a well-known source of cholesterol.

Cholesterol is never found in vegetable fats. It is made in the human body, and is, indeed essential to life and health, but the body can make it in excess from too many calories regardless of their sources. Heredity often plays an important part in blood and coronary problems. Persons with a family history of coronaries obviously should be even more careful than others how they live and what—and how much—they eat.

There is considerable evidence that certain vegetable oils, including safflower, corn, and soy (but not coconut or palm) are preferable to animal fats.* They are high in polyunsaturated fatty acids, quite the opposite of the fats from red meats and dairy products.

Other possible health hazards are much more difficult to determine, since a considerable amount of additional research is required. Many persons are concerned about a seeming correlation between meat eating and cancer; here the evidence to date is statistical and may be affected by other differences among the population groups studied. This evidence often involves the additional factor of sufficient fiber, or lack of it, in the diet.[7]

Certainly one of the most practical health-related reasons for vegetarianism is the opportunity to feast on nature's abundance of plant life. The imaginative vegetarian meal planner sees a variety of resources often bypassed by persons dependent on flesh foods for protein nutrition.

Religious Motives

Many religions have advocated, and a few have enforced, vegetarianism. The philosophies behind these customs include belief in reincarnation and the transmigration of souls, concepts of compassion, desire for mortification of the body and control of its lusts, and faith in man's original diet as recorded in Genesis, the first book in the bible. Thus, when we enter the religious and philosophical realm, the route becomes immensely complex.

Vegetarianism is not a requirement of the Seventh-day Adventist church, although abstinence from "unclean"

---

*Although a few seafoods, such as oysters, are high in cholesterol, fish oils are considered preferable to the fat of red meats.

meats, as defined in the Old Testament book of Leviticus, is strongly urged. Because of language and translation problems it is often difficult to determine which animals, fishes, and fowl were clean and which unclean. The pig, however, is invariably classed as unclean, along with scaleless and/or finless water creatures.

Lacto-ovo-vegetarianism is very actively promoted in official Seventh-day Adventist church publications, and by its ministers, physicians, dietitians, teachers, and others. Church and neighborhood cooking classes are held frequently. Emphasis in these classes is largely on meatless entrees, whole-grain and low-sugar cookery, and extensive use of fruits and vegetables. Seventh-day Adventist medical institutions generally offer patients a lacto-ovo-vegetarian diet program, with meat available for those who request it. No meat is served in employee cafeterias, nor to students in the church's schools, colleges, and universities. A number of public vegetarian restaurants are operated by Seventh-day Adventists.

Adventist reasons for vegetarianism include: (1) the original plant food diet assigned to all living creatures during creation week, according to the biblical account, (2) the suffering which is inflicted upon animals; (3) disease in food animals; (4) the effects of the killing and eating of animals on the mental and spiritual health of human beings; (5) the Christian's responsibility to maintain the highest level of physical and spiritual health. There is also much concern over world food problems, but the church's stand on vegetarianism precedes by many decades today's recognition of widespread danger of famine.

Another religious concept is that followed by the great monastic orders of the Catholic Church. "Mortification of the flesh," i.e., severe restriction on human appetites and desires, is believed to be conducive to religious experience. Sometimes such restrictions are used as penance for sins committed; in any case their purpose is to bring about a higher level of religious devotion. Abstinence from meat has been common among such restrictions.

The Order of Cistercians of the Strict Observance, popularly known as "Trappists," is a Roman Catholic religious order following a communal program of austerity patterned after the Benedictine rule. Silence, meditation and prayer, and daily manual labor comprise much of the penitential regimen which is the monk's life. Their diet includes vegetables, fruits, bread, and some milk and cheese. Meat and eggs are excluded.[8]

A study of Trappist monks in two monasteries in the United States was conducted to determine the effects of their diet and secluded lifestyle. Their intake of dairy products included small amounts of butter, about three cups of whole milk per man per day, and two ounces of cheese weekly. Eggs were permitted only in cases of illness. In spite of the relatively low intake of animal proteins the diet was not low in protein. Blood cholesterol levels were lower than those reported for corresponding American men.[9]

Traditionally, among the first foods to be given up by lay members of the Roman Catholic Church during temporary periods of fasting was meat. Here, however, a distinction has often been made between (red) meats and fish or poultry. Penitential abstinence was credited by St. Augustine with purifying the soul, raising the level of the mind, producing humility, destroying evil desires, and encouraging chastity. For this reason, and not because meat was intrinsically evil, the Church commanded abstinence at stated periods of time. Ecclesiastical authorization and Christian practice determined which flesh floods were forbidden. Although American Catholics no longer uniformly fast on Friday, abstinence from meat may be an act of penance.[10]

There are truly ancient religious beliefs which influence their followers to become vegetarians. One of the oldest is belief in the transmigration of souls—the almost endless perpetuation of life through reincarnation. The origin of this widespread belief is unknown, but it, or a closely related concept, still forms a basis for many of the religious and philosophical teachings of Hindus, Buddhists, Jains, and Theosophists.

The accompanying concept, *Karma*, has been called the keystone of the arch on which Hinduism has been erected.[11] It is the law of the inescapability of the results of one's actions in whatever life one is living. The next life, which follows the inevitable experience of reincarnation, will be pleasanter or more miserable according to the way the individual is living his present life. If he has fallen sufficiently short of a noble existence, he will enter the body of a lower order of life in his next rebirth. The soul of the righteous, on the other hand, moves to a higher level.

Added to the twin concepts of Karma and reincarnation is the ideal of *ahimsa*—nonviolence, doing no hurt to any living creature.[12] This ancient concept of *ahimsa* is, in essence, a strong factor in the current vegetarian movement in the United States. It means compassion for and kindness to animals, extending the golden rule to creatures who, although they cannot speak, nevertheless suffer pain and fear death as do humans.

The religion of the Jains has been described as one of love and kindness. Not only do the Jains refuse to destroy animal life, but they establish homes for aged and/or ailing animals. In these homes they feed and care for them until death comes naturally.[13]

In addition to formal religions promoting or practicing vegetarianism, the individual views of many famous historical figures noted for their philosophical contributions to the world of their day have come down to us. From Pythagoras and Empedocles of Grecian fame to Mahatma Gandhi, modern Indian apostle of freedom through nonviolence, they have left the stamp of their convictions on history.[14]

Naturally, vegetarian organizations came into existence. One is said to have been formed in Manchester, England, in 1809 when members of a Christian sect decided to give up flesh foods and alcoholic beverages. In the mid-1800s a vegetarian society was formed in the United States. Later such groups developed in Germany and France. By the 1960s there was an American Vegetarian Union and an American Vegan Society, both members of the International Vegetarian Union.[15] Today vegetarian programs are promoted by several dedicated organizations in many countries.

It was during the 1960s that vegetarianism suddenly made its presence felt in the United States. Genuine movements and extremist groups were soon confused in the public mind. Some pronounced the whole system dangerous to present and future generations. Finally, the smoke began to clear, as nutrition authorities and concerned organizations began alerting the public to the dangers inherent in extreme patterns of restriction and to the safety of scientifically validated vegetarianism.

References

1. R. Ferrando, "The Water Problem," in *World Review of Nutrition and Dietetics*, vol. 11, ed. Geoffrey H. Bourne (Basel, Switzerland and New York: S. Karger, 1969), pp. 17-45.

2. Charles C. Bradley, "Human Water Needs and Water Use in America," *Science* 138 (October 26, 1962): 489-91.

3. J. H. MacGillivray and J. B. Bosley, "Amino Acid Production per Acre by Plants and Animals," *Economic Botany* 16 (1962):25. Cited in Aaron M. Altschul, *Proteins, Their Chemistry and Politics* (New York: Basic Books, 1965), pp. 262-64.

4. Frances Moore Lappé; *Diet for a Small Planet*, rev. ed. (New York: Ballantine Books, 1975).

5. George Alexander, "Brown Rice as a Way of Life," *The New York Times Magazine* (March 2, 1972), pp. 89-104.

6. "The Zen Child," *Newsweek* 80 (September 18, 1972):71.

7. Denis Burkitt, "Food Fiber and Disease Prevention," *Comprehensive Therapy* 1 (September 1975):19-20; "Diet, Intestinal Flora, and Colon Cancer," *Nutrition Reviews* 33 (May 1975):136-37; and R. L. Phillips, "Role of Life-style and Dietary Habits in Risk of Cancer Among Seventh-day Adventists," *Cancer Research* (suppl) 35 (November 1975):3513-22.

8. *Collier's Encyclopedia* (1975), s.v. "Trappists"; Francis L. Filas, "Trappist," *The World Book Encyclopedia* (1977); *Encyclopedia Britannica* (1971), s.v. "Trappists" in "Cistercians."

9. E. Perry McCullagh and Lena A. Leives, "A Study of Diet, Blood Lipids and Vascular Disease in Trappist Monks," *The New England Journal of Medicine* 263 (September 22, 1960):569-74.

10. James D. Neill, "Abstinence," *The Catholic Encyclopedia* (1913); C. I. Litzinger, "Penance, Sacramental," *New Catholic Encyclopedia* (1967).

11. *Encyclopaedia Britannica*, (1971), s.v. "Karma;" Edmund Davison Soper, *The Religions of Mankind*, 3rd ed. rev. (Nashville, Tenn.: Abingdon Press, 1966), p. 98.

12. David T. Holland, "Pacifism," *Encyclopedia International* (1964); T. W. Rhys Davids, "Ahimsa," *Encylopaedia of Religion and Ethics* (1917).

13. *Encyclopaedia Britannica* (1971), s.v. "Jainism;" Hermann Jacobi, "Jainism," *Encyclopaedia of Religion and Ethics* (1915).

14. *Encyclopedia Americana* (1974), s.v. "Vegetarianism"; Joan V. Bondurant, "Gandhi, Mohandas Karamchand," *The World Book Encyclopedia* (1977).

15. *Encyclopedia Americana* (1974), s.v. "Vegetarianism."

Conclusion

It must, by now, have become quite obvious that we cannot say, "This is the reason people become vegetarians," though an individual may readily explain, "This is why *I* am a vegetarian."

In contrast to these numerous explanations for forgoing meat, we hear only two reasons for eating meat: its nutritive qualities and the liking most people have for it. In former centuries, of course, there was a third, and very compelling reason: the scarcity of any but animal resources in primitive, nonagricultural areas of the world.

In the technologically advanced countries of the West today, meat or no meat is a choice among life styles. Jean Mayer, outstanding nutrition authority, has said that if he is given an individual's personal reason for adopting a vegetarian diet, he can predict with a good chance of accuracy whether or not the diet will be adequate.[1] Dr. Mayer's chief concern is for persons refusing animal products for "health" reasons, since this is the area in which extremists can do maximum damage. At this point, of course, we are brought back to the pseudovegetarian programs which are not part of vegetarianism at all. For there is no reason why a genuine vegetarian diet should not be adequate—no reason, that is, except ignorance, or carelessness, or unfounded notions about food, or severe poverty, all of which can destroy with equal finality the adequacy of a meat diet.

Truly, Dr. Mayer has a valid concern. But knowledgeable vegetarians have a health standing at least as good as their nonvegetarian neighbors'. In the early 1900s the endurance records of vegetarian contestants surprised the American public. Today probably the most widely recognized group of vegetarians with lower death rates from certain types of cardiovascular disease and cancer are the Seventh-day Adventists.[2] In neither case are the reasons behind the records fully known.

And we should never forget that there are health requirements other than food: clean water, pure air, warm sunlight, pleasant relations with other humans and even animals, serene attitudes toward our environment, and trust in a Supreme Power to take care of our—and the world's—future.

"The life," said Christ, "is more than meat (food), and the body is more than raiment."[3]

We are not made up of lives, a physical life, a mental life, a spiritual life. Each of us is one life, in which the body—even the digestion—and the mind and the spirit must all work together, or all will suffer. Vegetarianism, as a self-chosen, wisely planned, and well-rounded regimen, can contribute much to this life.

References

1. Jean Mayer, "Can Man Live by Vegetables Alone?" *Family Health* 5: (February 1973): 32 ff.

2. Richard T. Walden, Louis E. Schaefer, Frank R. Lemon, Abraham Sunshine and Ernest L. Wynder, "Effect of Environment on the Serum Cholesterol-triglyceride Distribution among Seventh-day Adventists," *American Journal of Medicine* 36 (February 1964): 269-76; Roland L. Phillips, "Role of Life-style and Dietary Habits in Risk of Cancer among Seventh-day Adventists," *Cancer Research* 35 (November 1975): 3513-22; and Frank R. Lemon and Jan W. Kuzma, "A Biologic Cost of Smoking," *Archives of Environmental Health* 18 (June 1969): 950-55.

3. Luke 12:23, KJV.

Appendix A

Sample Menus
for a Week

The following menus are examples only. It is not expected that every individual or every family will use or enjoy them. Many, many other combinations are possible.

Foods on the pure vegetarian menu are similar to those on the lacto-ovo vegetarian samples. Substitutions are suggested wherever eggs or dairy products appear. An asterisk (*) indicates that the recipe is included in the Appendix.

The menus have been carefully calculated for adequacy (RDAs for adults) of the major nutrients: proteins, calcium, iron, vitamins A and C, thiamin, riboflavin, and niacin. The vitamin and mineral values meet the RDAs and in most cases are well above the recommended allowances.

The calories range from 2100 to 2300 a day. The recommended daily allowance for calories is 2100 for the adult woman and 2700 for the adult man. The servings can be varied according to age, size and weight. The daily protein requirement is 46 grams for women and 56 grams for men. The protein ranges from 60 to 80 grams a day. The fat content has been planned to stay within 25 percent of the total calories.

Amounts are listed on menus in order to make accurate calculations. The abbreviations used are C. = cup, tsp. = teaspoon, T. = tablespoon.

97

Meal pattern:	*Lacto-ovo vegetarian*	*Pure vegetarian*
	1st day	*1st day*
BREAKFAST	Grapefruit half	Same
	½ C. oatmeal with dates	Same
	2 whole wheat toast	Same
	2 tsp. margarine	Same
	½ C. lowfat milk	Soymilk (fortified)
LUNCH OR SUPPER	Split pea soup	Same
	2 cornbread	Same (omit egg)
	2 tsp. margarine	Same
	Fresh fruit-banana	Same
	1 C. nonfat milk	Soymilk
DINNER	2 enchiladas*	Same
	Spanish rice* (use brown rice)	Same
	Tossed salad (lettuce, tomatoes,	Same
	cucumbers)	Same
	1 T. french dressing	Same
	½ C. prunes	Same
	1 C. orange-pineapple juice	Same
	2nd day	*2nd day*
BREAKFAST	1 C. orange juice	Same
	4 buckwheat pancakes with	Same (make with soymilk,
	1 C. applesauce and	Same omit egg)
	¼ C. cottage cheese	Almonds
	¼ C. postum with milk (lowfat	Same (use soymilk)
	if desired)	
LUNCH OR SUPPER	Avocado, tomato, lettuce	
	sandwich	Same
	2/3 C. bean salad*	Same
	2 sl. pineapple	Same
	¼ C. hot beverage with	Same
	¼ cup lowfat milk	
DINNER	Soy chicken	Cashew nuts
	Brown rice with curry sauce	Same (Sauce made with
	(made with 1 cup	Same 1 cup soymilk).
	lowfat milk).	
	Green peas, Diced apple,	Same
	Raisins—serve on top of rice	Same
	Melon	Same
	1 whole wheat roll	Same

Meal pattern:	Lacto-ovo vegetarian	Pure vegetarian
	3rd day	*3rd day*
BREAKFAST	1 orange sliced	Same
	1 C. multi-grain cooked cereal with	Same
	raisins, ½ cup lowfat	Same
	milk	Soymilk
	2 whole wheat toast	Same
	2 tsp. margarine	Same
	1 C. lowfat milk	Soymilk
LUNCH OR		
SUPPER	2 tacos filled with:	Same
	Beans	Same
	Lettuce	Same
	Tomatoes	Same
	Grated lowfat cheese	Omit cheese; use chopped nuts
	Fresh fruit—strawberries	Same
	Nonfat milk	Soymilk
	1 fruit bar	Same
DINNER	Mushroom omelet (using 1 egg)	Browned Tofu with mushrooms*
	1 lge. baked potato	Same
	½ C. string beans	Same
	Sliced tomato and spinach salad	Same
	2 whole wheat rolls	Same
	1 tsp. margarine	Same
	1 baked apple with raisins	Same
	Fruit Punch	Same
	4th day	*4th day*
BREAKFAST	Grapefruit juice	Same
	2 whole wheat toast with	Same
	2 T. peanut butter and	Same
	5 dates	Same
	Hot beverage with ¼ cup lowfat milk	Hot beverage
LUNCH OR		
SUPPER	Corn chowder with	Same (make with soymilk)
	croutons-made with lowfat milk	Same
	Coleslaw	Same
	Sandwich (shredded carrots,	Same
	nuts, raisins)	Same
	Tomato juice	Same
	Fresh fruit cup	Same
DINNER	Mushroom-Lima Bake*	Same
	Baked sweet potato	Same
	Broccoli	Same
	1 Fruit Bar*	Same
	Lowfat milk	Soymilk

Meal pattern:	*Lacto-ovo vegetarian*	*Pure vegetarian*
	5th day	*5th day*
BREAKFAST	Whole orange	Same
	Whole wheat cereal	Same
	1 slice Prosage (meat analog)	Same
	Multigrain toast	Same
	1 C. lowfat milk	Soymilk
	Hot beverage	
LUNCH OR SUPPER	Vegeburger patties* in	Same
	whole wheat bun with	Same
	tomatoes	Same
	mayonnaise	Margarine
	Apple	Same
	Pineapple-Apricot Nectar	
DINNER	Lentil Roast*	Same
	Creamed potatoes and peas	Same
	Turnip greens	Same
	Relishes: carrots, celery,	Same
	radishes	Same
	2 corn muffins	Same
	Margarine	Same
	Grape Juice	Same
	6th day	*6th day*
BREAKFAST	1 C. orange juice	Same
	2 Almond Oat Waffles*	Same
	½ C. blueberry sauce	Same
	1 C. lowfat milk	Soymilk
LUNCH OR SUPPER	Baked beans	Same
	Sliced tomatoes and lettuce	Same
	2 whole wheat rolls	Same
	2 tsp. margarine	Same
	2 Date-Oatmeal Cookies*	Fruit Bars*
		Soymilk
DINNER	Lasagna*	Glutenburger Loaf
	1 corn on cob	Same
	Tossed green salad	Same
	2 toasted garlic bread (enriched)	Same
	1 tsp. margarine	Same
	Stewed apricots	Same

Meal pattern:	*Lacto-ovo vegetarian*	*Pure vegetarian*
	7th day	*7th day*
BREAKFAST	½ C. fresh peaches	Same
	½ C. Granola*	Same
	1½ C. lowfat milk	Soymilk
	2 Whole wheat toast	Same
	2 tsp. margarine	Same
	Hot beverage	
LUNCH OR		
SUPPER	Fresh fruit salad on lettuce	Same
	½ C. cottage cheese	Omit cheese
	4 prunes	Add nuts and seeds
	Whole wheat bread sticks	Same
		Soymilk
DINNER	Pecan balls in mushroom gravy*	Soy-oat patties with tomato sauce*
	Baked stuffed potato	Same
	Carrots	Same
	Green salad and 1 T. french dressing	Same
	Whole wheat roll	Same
	Apple pie with whole wheat crust	Same

Recipes

**Indicates recipe from *The Oats, Peas, Beans and Barley Cookbook*, by Edyth Young Cottrell (Santa Barbara, Calif.: Woodbridge Press, 1978).

*Almond-Oat Waffles***

2¼ cups water
1½ cups rolled oats
⅓ cup almonds
¼ cup wheat germ

1 tablespoon oil
1 tablespoon sugar
½ teaspoon salt

Combine all ingredients and blend until light and foamy, about half a minute. Let stand while waffle iron is heating. The batter thickens on standing. Blend briefly.

Grease iron with solid shortening for first waffle. (Do not use margarine.) Bake in hot waffle iron 8 to 10 minutes, or until nicely browned. Set timer (or check time carefully by the clock) for 8 minutes and do not open before time is up. If waffle iron is hard to open, leave a few seconds longer.

*Lentil Roast***

2 cups cooked lentils	½ cup Brazil nuts, chopped
1 cup cooked rice	1 ⅓ teaspoons brewer's yeast
1 cup soaked garbanzos	1 teaspoon salt, or to taste
½ cup water	½ teaspoon sage

Measure lentils into a bowl. Add rice. Blend garbanzos with water until fine and add to lentils and rice. Add chopped nuts and seasonings.

Bake in oiled baking dish or casserole 350° F., 45 minutes (covered for first 30 minutes, uncovered for last 15 minutes).

Garnish with parsley and strips of pimiento or red bell pepper and serve. Serves six.

*Vegeburger Patties***

1 cup vegetarian "burger"	½ cup sautéed onions
1 cup soaked garbanzos	½ teaspoon salt
½ cup water	½ teaspoon sage
2 tablespoons wheat germ	1 tablespoon oil

Measure vegeburger into a mixing bowl. Blend soaked garbanzos in water. Add to vegeburger. Add remaining ingredients. Mix well. Shape into patties. Bake in lightly oiled covered skillet at 350° F., 10 minutes. Turn. Cover. Bake an additional 10 minutes. Serves six.

Soy-Oat Patties with Tomato Sauce**

The Patties:

1 cup soaked soybeans	¼ teaspoon onion powder
½ cup water	Speck garlic powder
2 tablespoons flake yeast or	1 teaspoon Italian seasoning
1 tablespoon powdered yeast	½ teaspoon salt (or to taste)
1 tablespoon soy sauce	⁵/₈ cups rolled oats, regular
1 tablespoon oil	

Combine all ingredients except rolled oats in blender and chop fine; or, beans may be ground in a food chopper and combined with other ingredients. Place in bowl. Add rolled oats and let stand 10 minutes to absorb moisture.

Drop from tablespoon or half-cup scoop on oiled baking pan or electric skillet. Cover.

Bake at 350°F. for 10 minutes until nicely browned. Turn. Cover and bake additional 10 minutes. Reduce heat and cook 10 minutes more. Serve with Tomato Sauce. Yields 4 2-patty servings.

Tomato Sauce:

2 cups cooked tomatoes	1 tablespoon sugar
½ cup sautéed onions	½ teaspoon salt
½ cup chopped green pepper	1 teaspoon sweet basil
1 tablespoon oil	

Add sautéed onions and chopped pepper to juice of tomatoes in sauce pan and bring to boil. Let simmer until reduced about half in volume. Cut tomatoes in small pieces or mash and add with seasoning to juice. Let simmer briefly. (Should be quite thick.) Serve over patties.

*Fruit Bars***

2½ cups rolled oats
½ cup whole wheat pastry flour
1 tablespoon brown sugar

2 tablespoons soy flour
½ teaspoon salt
⅓ cup oil
⅓ cup water

Measure into bowl. Measure water and oil in cup. Beat with fork until oil is moistened evenly. Let stand while preparing Filling.

Filling:

1½ cups dates, raisins,
 or combination
½ cup water

¼ teaspoon salt
½ cup chopped nuts
1 tablespoon lemon juice

Grind raisins or chop in blender with water. Combine with chopped dates and nuts. Add salt and lemon juice. Mix well. Mix oat mixture well with fork or fingers.

Flatten a little less than half into bottom of greased 8" × 8" pan. Press down firmly with fingers. Spread filling evenly over crust. Put remaining mixture over filling. Press firmly with fingers or fork.

Bake at 375° F. for 25-30 minutes or until a delicate brown. Cool before removing from pan. Loosen edges, invert pan on cloth-covered tray by putting tray on top of pan and turning over. Pat sharply on bottom of pan. Cut in 2" squares. Makes 16 squares.

Date-Oatmeal Cookies**

1 cup dates	½ teaspoon salt
½ cup water	1 teaspoon vanilla
1 cup shredded raw apple	¼ cup chopped dates
¾ cup oil	3 cups rolled oats
½ cup chopped walnuts	

Combine dates and water in saucepan. Heat, mash, and stir until smooth.

Add shredded apple and oil and beat until smooth and oil is emulsified. Add other ingredients. Mix well. Let stand 10 minutes to absorb moisture. Beat briskly.

Drop from teaspoon on ungreased cookie sheet. Bake at 375°F. 25 minutes or until nicely browned. Yield: 36 cookies.

Bean Salad

1 cup kidney beans	½ cup lemon juice
1 cup green beans	¼ cup brown sugar
1 cup garbanzos	1 stalk celery
2 tablespoons oil	¼ cup onions

Mix all ingredients together; do not mash beans.

Spoon into serving dish. Lay onion rings on top, if desired. Cover and refrigerate overnight.

Lasagna

1 clove garlic, crushed
1 cup onion, chopped
½ cup oil
1 14-ounce can gluten burger
½ teaspoon salt, or to taste
3½ cups (No. 2½ can) tomatoes
1 8-ounce can tomato sauce
1 teaspoon oregano
1 teaspoon sweet basil
½ teaspoon thyme

½ cup chopped parsley
(or 2 tablespoons dried
parsley flakes)
8 ounces lasagna noodles
(wide) uncooked
2 cups (1 pound) creamed
cottage cheese (or
one pound ricotta cheese)
8 ounces mozzarella cheese,
sliced thin

Sauté onion and garlic in oil. Add burger and salt and brown slightly.

Combine all ingredients except noodles and cheese, and simmer sauce about 1 hour. Cook noodles as directed on package; drain.

Arrange alternate layers of sauce, 2 layers of noodles crisscrossed, cottage cheese, and mozzarella in buttered 11″× 7″ baking dish.

Repeat layers, ending with sauce.

Bake for 30 minutes at 375°F. Let stand about 10 minutes in warm place before serving. Yields 8 servings.

Spanish Rice

2 cups water
1 teaspoon oil
1 onion, minced
1 cup raw brown rice
½ cup celery, diced small
1 large green pepper, diced

1 cup canned tomatoes, chopped
1 teaspoon salt
½ teaspoon oregano
½ teaspoon basil
½ cup grated lowfat
or jack cheese (optional)

Bring the water with oil, onions, and rice to a boil. Cover and simmer on low heat for 25 minutes. Add remaining ingredients except cheese. Simmer another 20 minutes or until rice is well cooked. Sprinkle cheese on top if desired. Makes 4 cups.

Enchiladas

Sauce:

2 tablespoons oil
1 cup onions, chopped
2 cups canned tomatoes
1 8-ounce can tomato sauce

1 clove garlic, minced
½ teaspoon salt

Sauté onions in oil. Add to other ingredients. Simmer, uncovered, for 30 minutes.

Filling:

1½ cups mashed cooked pinto beans
½ cup onions, sautéed and chopped
½ cup black olives, chopped
¼ teaspoon salt

Stir ingredients together well.

¼ pound lowfat cheese, grated
Black olive halves
8 soft corn tortillas

To assemble: Fill tortillas with 2-3 tablespoons of filling and 1 tablespoon of grated cheese. Place, rolled up, in a shallow baking pan. Cover with sauce, sprinkle with cheese, and garnish with olive halves. Bake at 350°F. for 30 minutes until bubbling hot.

Granola

7 cups oats	½ cup brown sugar
1 cup wheat germ	½ cup water
1 cup coconut, shredded	½ cup oil
1 cup nuts (cashews and almonds)	1 teaspoon salt
1 cup sunflower seeds	1 tablespoon vanilla

Mix dry ingredients well. Place liquids in bowl and beat until emulsified. Combine all ingredients together. Place on cookie sheet, spread evenly. Bake at 275° for 1-1½ hours; stir every half hour with a pancake turner.

Browned Tofu with Mushrooms

1½ pounds tofu (soy cheese)	1 package Gravy Quik*
1 cup onion, chopped	1½ cups water
2 tablespoons oil	2 tablespoons soy sauce
1 4-ounce can sliced mushrooms	1 teaspoon monosodium glutamate
	½ cup green onions, chopped

Steam or simmer tofu for 20 minutes. Drain tofu and cut in 1½-inch squares and brown on baking sheet in hot (400°F.) oven for 20 minutes. Sauté onion in oil five minutes; add mushrooms. Prepare Gravy Quik, mix with water, soy sauce, and monosodium glutamate and add to sautéed onions.

Cook over low heat until thickened. Mix all ingredients together except green onions. Bake in buttered baking dish at 350°F. for 40 minutes. Sprinkle green onions over top before serving. Serves six.

---

*Loma Linda Foods low calorie gravy mix.

Mushroom-Lima Bake

1 package frozen baby lima beans
1 medium onion, sliced thin
½ pound fresh mushrooms, sliced
2 tablespoons salad oil
½ can cream of mushroom soup
½ teaspoon salt
¼ cup milk (or soymilk)

Cook beans in small amount of water for five minutes. Sauté onion and mushrooms in oil until vegetables are limp. Add onions, mushrooms, soup and salt to beans. Turn into greased casserole. Pour milk over top. Bake, covered, 30 to 40 minutes at 375°F.

Pecan Balls in Mushroom Gravy

2 cans mushrooms soup
½ cup water
½ cup sour cream
3 tablespoons parsley, chopped
⅓ cup milk
3 cups prepared bread stuffing
1½ cup pecans, chopped
½ cup lowfat cheese, grated
3 tablespoons onion, finely chopped
2 eggs, beaten

Prepare sauce of mushroom soup, water, milk, and sour cream. Set aside. Combine remaining ingredients and shape into 12 patties. Place in buttered casserole and cover with mushroom sauce. Top generously with more grated cheese and bake uncovered in a 350°F. oven for 30 minutes. Serves 6-8.

Glutenburger Loaf

2 cups glutenburger
¼ cup oil
½ cup onions, chopped
½ teaspoon salt
3 shredded wheat biscuits
1 cup nuts, chopped
1 teaspoon sage
1½ cups water or soy milk

Mix all ingredients together. Place in oiled loaf pan. Bake at 350°F. for one hour or until loaf is firm.

Appendix B

Suggestions for Dining Away from Home

Full-fledged vegetarian restaurants

These eating places are usually small, often relatively inexpensive, sometimes with a strong religious or philosophical emphasis such as the universal brotherhood of all living creatures.

Restaurants catering to cultural food tastes

Chinese, Greek, Italian, Mexican and other restaurants often include vegetarian dishes.

Cafeterias

A variety of choices may include one vegetarian entree. Other protein foods often include cottage cheese alone or in salads; legumes and nuts. Fruit, an assortment of salads and more than one vegetable will be available.

Smorgasbords

A popular type of buffet with several vegetarian food choices.

Restaurants

Choices vary according to size of the restaurant, clientele, etc. Possibilities include vegetable plates (which may not be featured on the menu), hot plates on request with vegetables and cottage cheese or other simple substitute for the entree; enough a la carte items to make a meal; special vegetarian salads with hearty arrangements of fresh vegetables, cheese, sprouts, etc. or salad bars where the customer serves himself. Generally a limited number of attractive items are featured at various times: fruit-cottage cheese plates or bowls, cheese sandwiches, omelets, waffles, etc. Meal accompaniments such as bacon and sausage will be omitted upon request.

Salad Bars

Salad bars are a new kind of dining establishment catering to dieters, natural food enthusiasts—and vegetarians. They offer a wide variety of salads, salad "makings" and accompaniments like soup and rolls, or possibly sandwiches.

Airlines

Most airlines serve vegetarian meals provided they are ordered in advance. Some airlines offer a choice of total vegetarian or lacto-ovo-vegetarian menus.

Supermarket meals

Fairly healthful meals can be obtained for eating "on the road" or even in one's hotel room (not inflicted on the maid who must clean the room afterward). There are whole grain breads and crackers, fruit (date or banana) breads, graham crackers, perhaps crunchy, not-too-sweet cereals to eat out of the package, nuts and nut butters, mild cheeses, fresh fruits, ready-to-eat dried fruits, unsweetened fruit juices, vegetable juices, milk and plain or fruit-flavored yogurt.

Appendix C

A Sampling of Vegetarian Cookbooks

Cookbooks are not necessarily also nutrition books, although some cookbook authors attempt to combine the two, and frequently succeed in doing so. All too often, however, a book containing excellent vegetarian recipes is less than scientifically accurate in the nutrition claims made or implied. Because of the need for delectable and creative recipes, we are ignoring the hazard of an occasional nutritional misstatement or exaggeration, and basing our selection process on the quality of the bulk of recipes included in the book. We leave determination of the accuracy of any stated or implied nutrition standards to the user. We hope that *A Vegetarian Diet* will help the reader to make correct judgments in such cases. In the meantime, we put no stamp of approval on any book listed herein, and offer our sincere appreciation to those authors who have done an excellent job of presenting nutrition facts with their recipes.

Neither do we recommend every recipe therein. Some vegetarians, the authors among them, use little sugar or honey and few or no spices. Many, including the authors, use neither wine nor caffeine beverages. Many people must restrict their intake of dairy fats and eggs. Again, for the sake of the many nutritious and tasty recipes which they contain, we are including a wide range of cookbooks.

Adventures in Vegetarian Cooking. J. J. Thurman. Southern Publishing Company, Nashville, Tenn., 1969.

An Apple a Day: Vegetarian Cookery by Doctors' Wives. Women's Auxiliary to the Alumni Association, Loma Linda University, School of Medicine. Typecraft, Inc., Pasadena, Calif., 1967.

Better Meals for Less. George Cornforth. Review and Herald Publishing Association, Washington, D.C., 1930.

Callaloo and Pastelles Too. Ruth B. Adams. Pacific Press Publishing Association, Mountain View, Calif., 1973.

Diet for a Small Planet, rev. ed. Frances Moore Lappé. New York: Ballantine Books, 1975.

Dining Delightfully: Tested Recipes from Adventist Hospital Chefs. Review and Herald Publishing Association, Washington, D.C., 1968.

Eat for Strength. Cookbook, Yuchi Pines Institute, Seale, Ala., n.d.

Entree Encores, Soup Encores, Vegetable Encores (3 pamphlets). Seventh-day Adventist Dietetic Association, Loma Linda, Calif., 1963, 1964.

Fifty-two Sabbath Menus. Jeanne Larson and Ruth A. McLin. Southern Publishing Association, Nashville, Tenn., 1969.

Forget-About-Meat Cookbook, The. Karen Brooks. Rodale Press, Inc., Emmaus, Pa., 1974.

Good Foods for Good Health. Thelma Bruner Harris. Southern Publishing Association, Nashville, Tenn., 1972.

Happy Living Cookbook. Jan Worth. Worthington Foods, Worthington, Ohio, 1974.

International Vegetarian Cookery. Sonya Richmond. Arco Publishing Company, Inc., New York, 1965.

It's Your World Vegetarian Cookbook. Seventh-day Adventist Church, Glendale, Calif., 1973.

Laurel's Kitchen, A Handbook for Vegetarian Cookery and Nutrition. Laurel Robertson, Carol Flinders, and Bronwen Godfrey. Nilgiri Press, Berkeley, Calif., 1976.

Meatless Recipes. Mattie Louise. Theosophical Publishing House, Wheaton, Ill., 1975.

Nature's Harvest. Darlene Prusia and Joanne Mohr. M and M Printers, College Place, Wash., 1977.

Oats, Peas, Beans and Barley Cookbook, The. Edyth Young Cottrell. Woodbridge Press Publishing Company, Santa Barbara, Calif., 1978.

Recipes for a Small Planet. Ellen Buchman Ewald. New York: Ballantine Books, 1973.

Recipes for Long Life, The Low Cholesterol Cookbook for Weight Conscious Vegetarians. Loma Linda Foods, Riverside, Calif., n.d.

RX Recipes: A Manual of Healthful Cookery. D. and L. Rosenwald. Outdoor Pictures, Escondido, Calif., 1963.

Soul to Soul: A Vegetarian Soul Food Cookbook. Mary Burgess. Woodbridge Press Publishing Company, Santa Barbara, Calif., 1976.

Soybean Cookbook, The. Dorthea Van Gundy Jones. Arco Publishing Company, Inc., New York, 1973.

Ten Talents. Frank J. and Rosalie Hurd. The College Press, Collegedale, Tenn., 1968.

375 Meatless Recipes, Century 21 Cookbook. Ethel Nelson, Leominster, Mass., 1974.

Vegetarian Cookery (5 books). Patricia Hall Black and Ruth Little Carey. Pacific Press Publishing Association, Mountain View, Calif., 1971. Book 1: *Appetizers, Salads, Beverages;* Book 2: *Breads, Soups, Sandwiches*; Book 3: *Main Dishes, Vegetables*; Book 4: *Desserts*; and Book 5: *Candies and Confections, Cooking for a Crowd.*

Vegetarian Epicure, The. Anna Thomas. Vintage Books, Division of Random House, New York, 1972.

Vegetarian Gourmet Cookery. Alan Hooker. 101 Productions, San Francisco, Calif. Distributed to the book trade by Charles Scribner's Sons, New York, 1970.

Meat Analog Manufacturers

Although a number of companies were, at one time, interested in the manufacture of textured vegetable protein and meat analogs, relatively few are currently engaged in producing ready-to-eat or other meat alternates for retail trade. A search for names and locations of such companies produced the following list, which may be incomplete:

Archer, Daniels, Midlands Company
Box 1470
Decatur, IL 62525

> Makers of Textured Vegetable Protein bases for use in food preparation. Sold only in bulk, may be packaged and sold by retail markets.

Cedar Lake Foods
P. O. Box 116
Cedar Lake, MI 48810

   Makers of canned meat analogs.

General Mills
Food Service and Bakery Mix Products
Minneapolis, MN 55440

   Makers of Baco chips and Baco bits, bacon-like products for use in hot foods, salads, sandwiches, etc.

Loma Linda Foods
11503 Pierce Street
Riverside, CA 92505

   Makers of a large line of canned, dehydrated, and
   frozen meat analogs under Loma Linda and La Loma
   labels.

Miles Laboratories
900 Proprietors Road
Worthington, OH 43085

   Makers of (1) a large line of frozen and canned meat
   analogs under the general title of Worthington Foods,
   and (2) a line of frozen meat analogs under the Morn-
   ingstar Farms brand.

Millstone Foods
Box 323
Penryn, CA 95663

   Makers of a limited but well-liked line of meat analogs.